YOUR TASK is to be ADMIRED

Photos & Stories

CATHRYN WELLNER

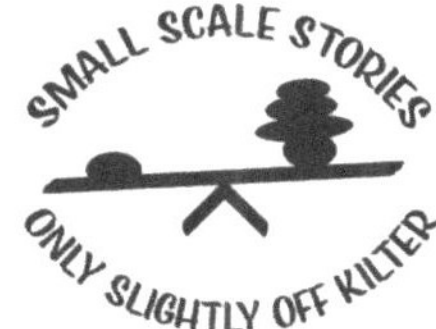

Small Scale Stories #5

Espoir Press

British Columbia 2017

Espoir Press
1002 - 1128 Sunset Drive
Kelowna, British Columbia
Canada V1Y 9W7

©2017 Cathryn Wellner

Your Task Is To Be Admired (Small Scale Stories #5)

ISBN 978-1-988760-08-7

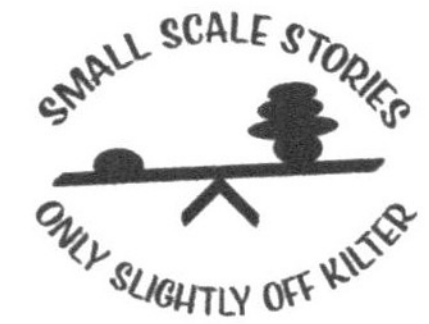

YOU ARE CREATIVE & INSPIRED

Your imagination is a theater with a full cast of characters. They compete for your attention. Some praise your intelligence and wit. Others shred your sense of self-worth. Some call you creative or inspiring. Others recite your failures.

In *Your Task Is To Be Admired*, those inner characters pull on disguises and tell their stories. They speak as flowers, birds, logs, water and even a slice of bread. Like the iris in this book, their only task is to be admired, but they stumble around in a labyrinth of emotions. One moment they dance with wild joy. The next they fall into a pit of despair.

These characters live inside everyone, but not everyone knows how to be entertained by their stories without being trashed by them. If you listen to seagulls, dance with wind, or play games with fish, you have the what it takes to enjoy their shenanigans without letting them call the shots.

You are creative and inspired. This book is for you.

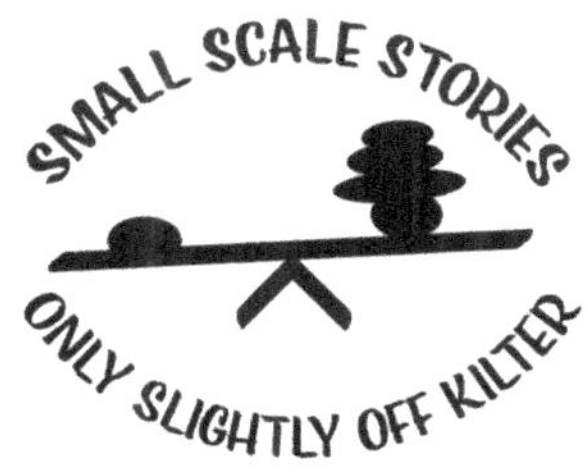

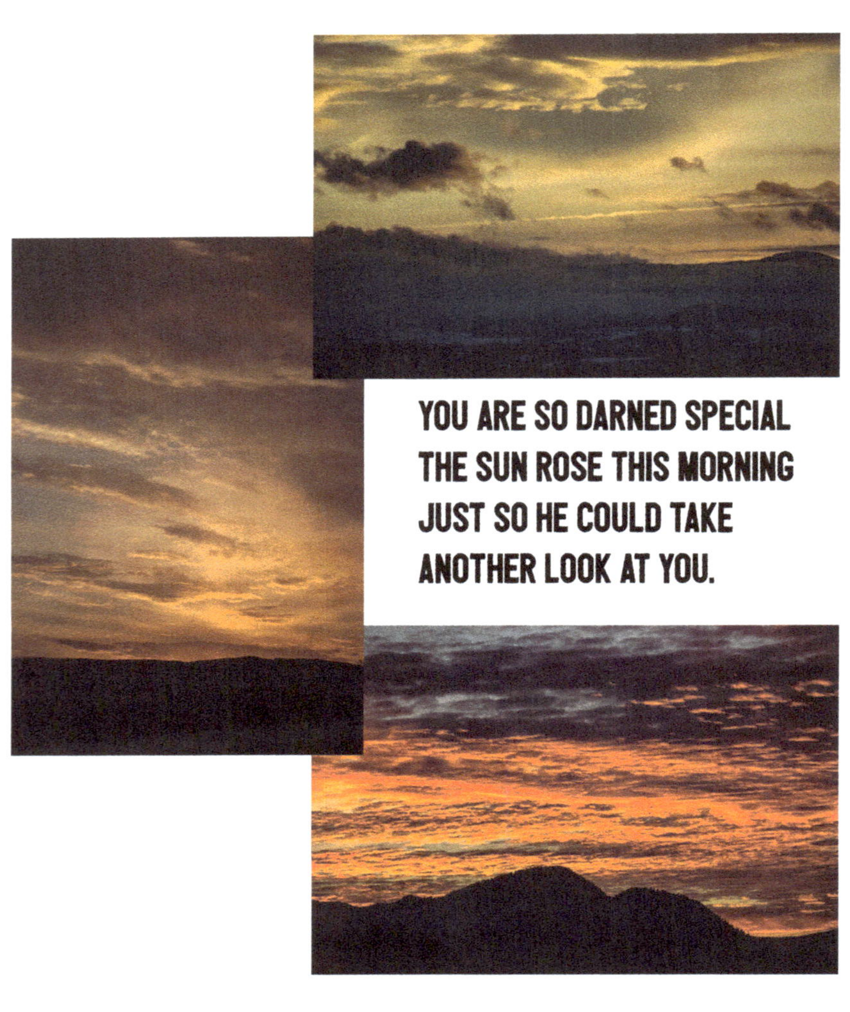
YOU ARE SO DARNED SPECIAL
THE SUN ROSE THIS MORNING
JUST SO HE COULD TAKE
ANOTHER LOOK AT YOU.

To all the beautiful people
who love the feel of sunshine
on their backs

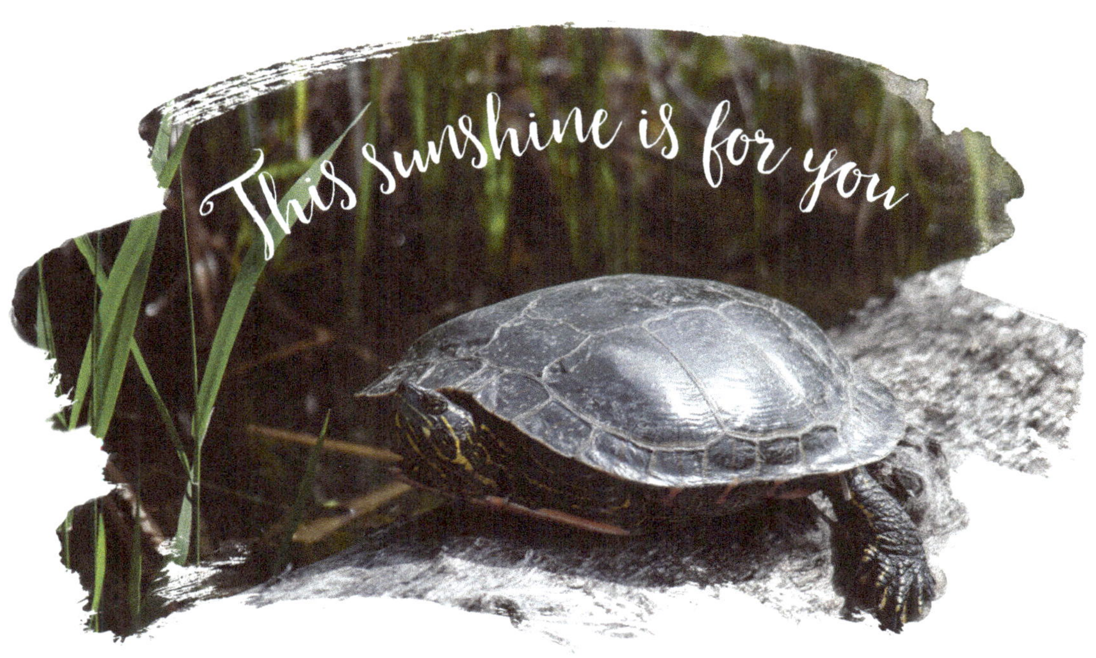

THE STORIES

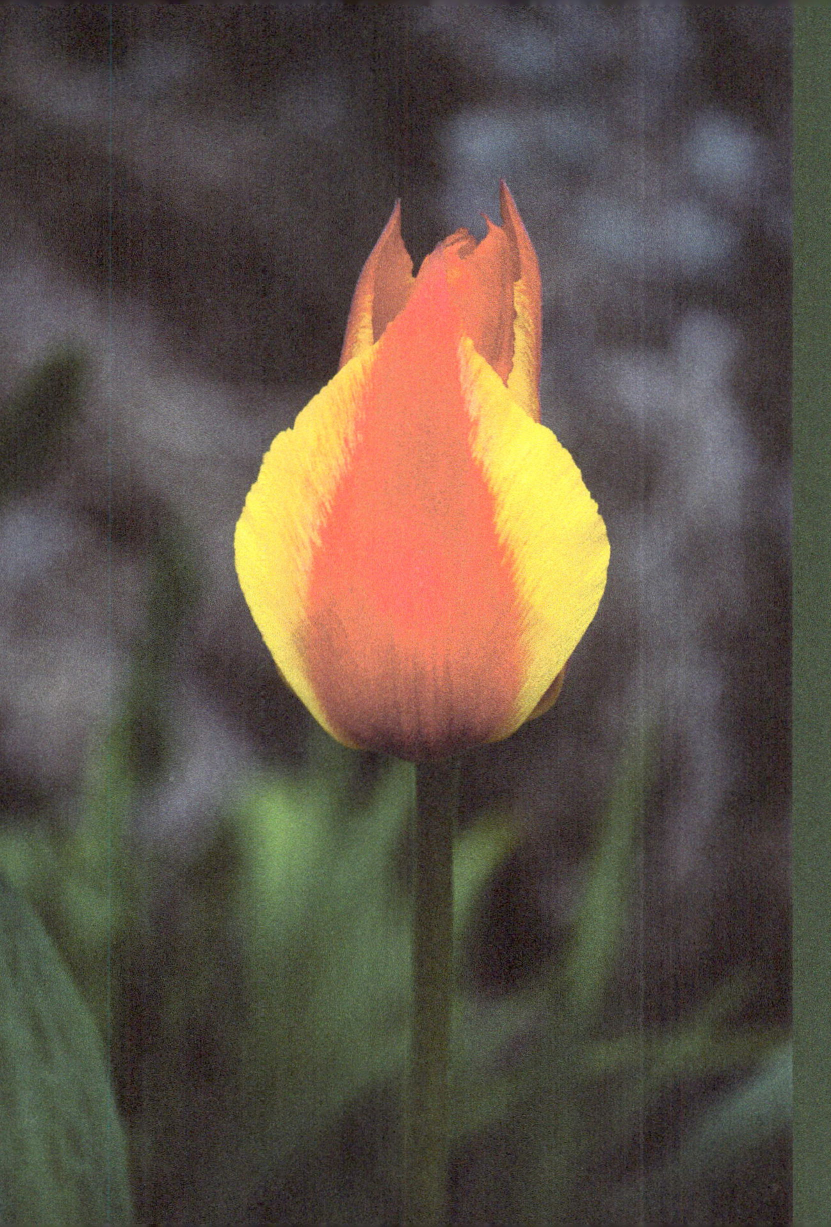

Harry decided to try a Darth Vader look this year, but when his petals began to unfold, he loved their bright colors and celebrated the failure of his plan.

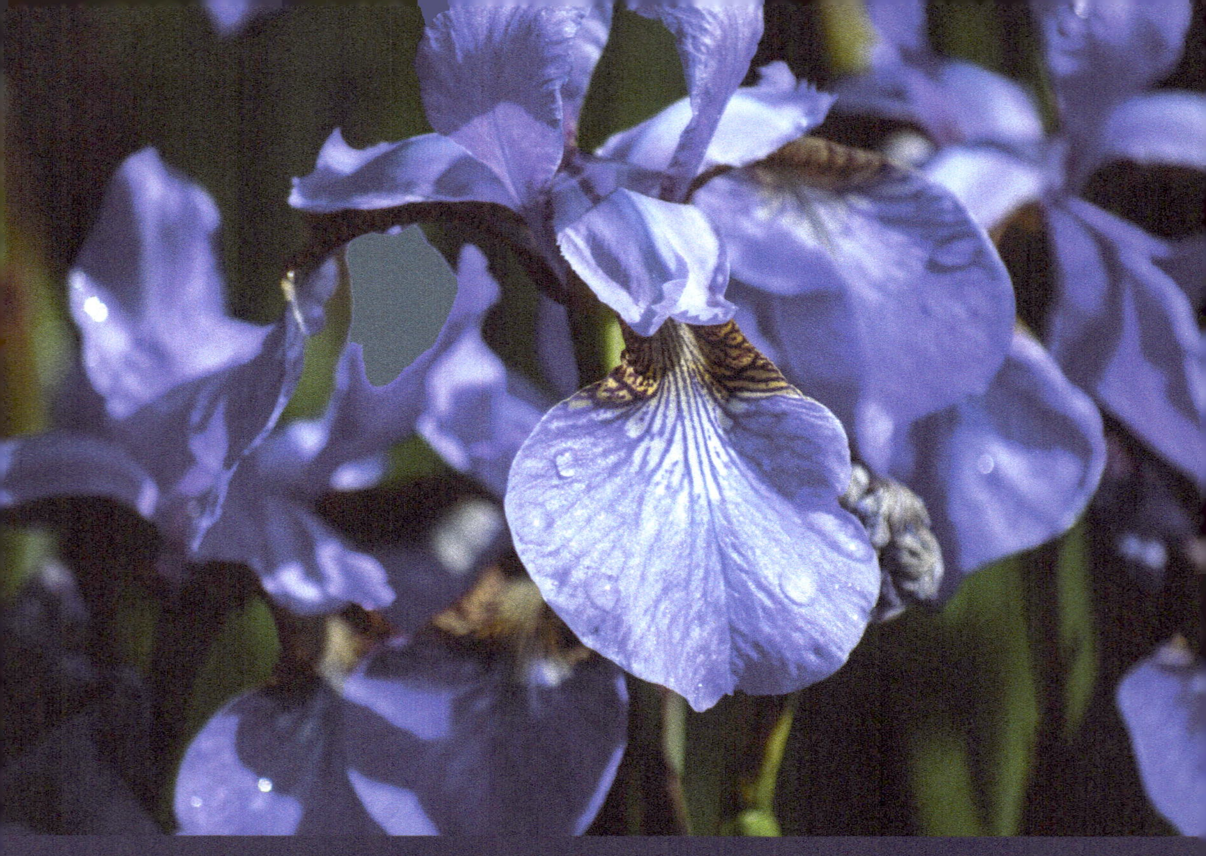

Fresh from her dewy bath, Iris eagerly awaited her day's work, being admired by everyone who passed through the garden.

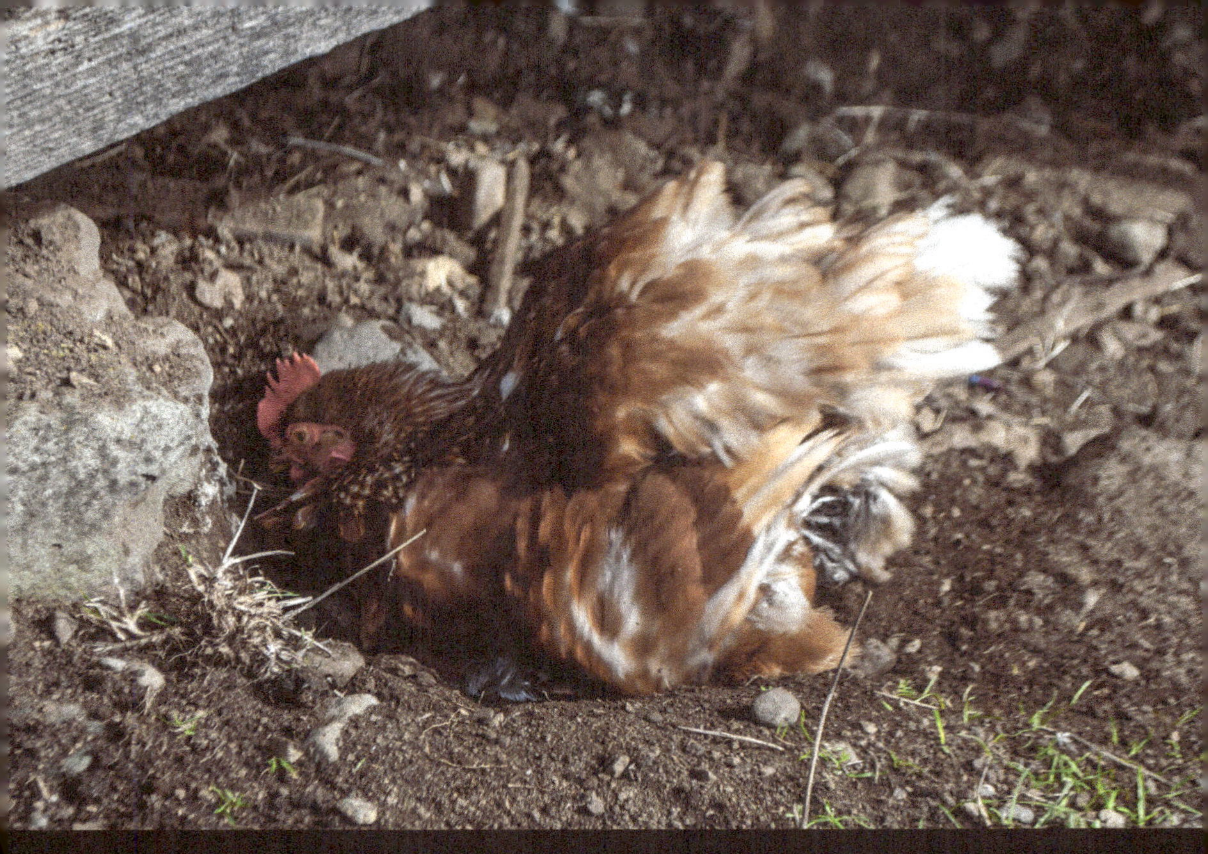

"Wait until he sees me after my dust bath," thought Hen. "Rooster won't be able to resist me."

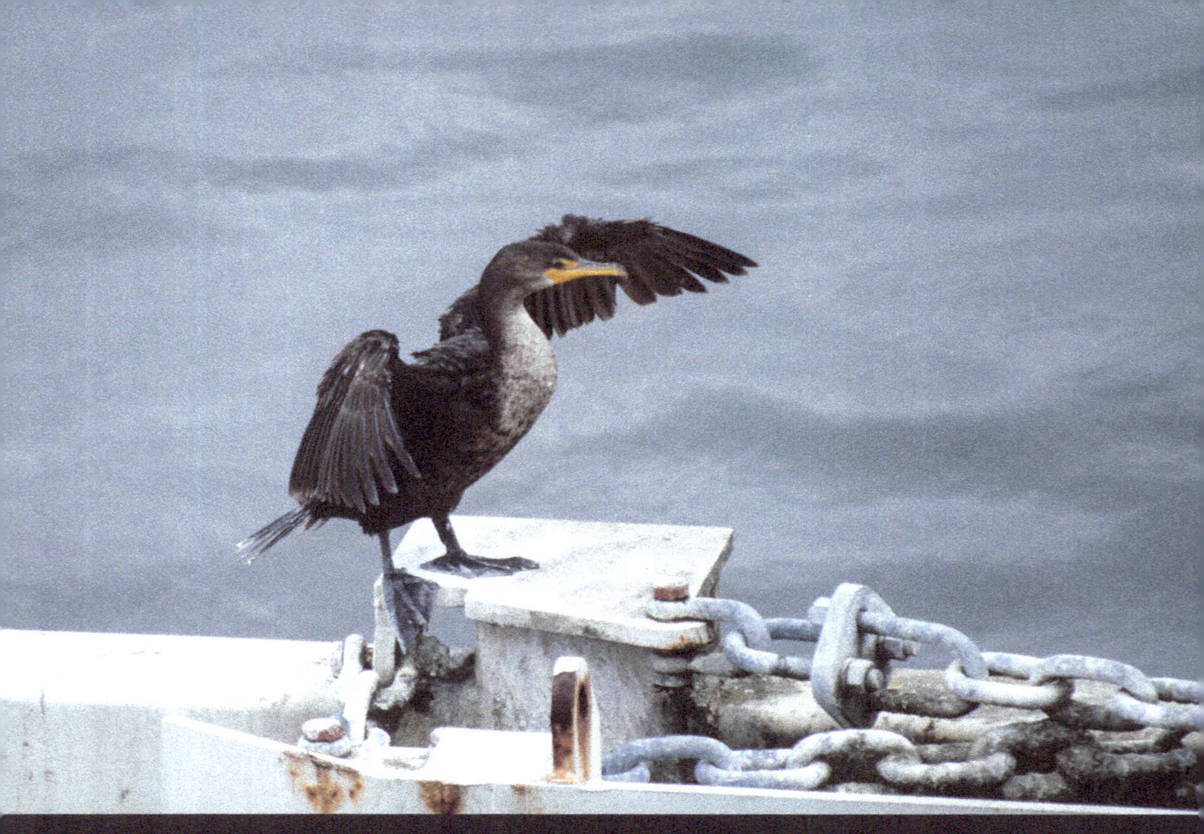

"Come on, Wind, dry my wings right now. I've got fishing to do." Even on sunny days Cormorant was not patient. On rainy days he wished Wind were a fish so he could threaten to gobble him down.

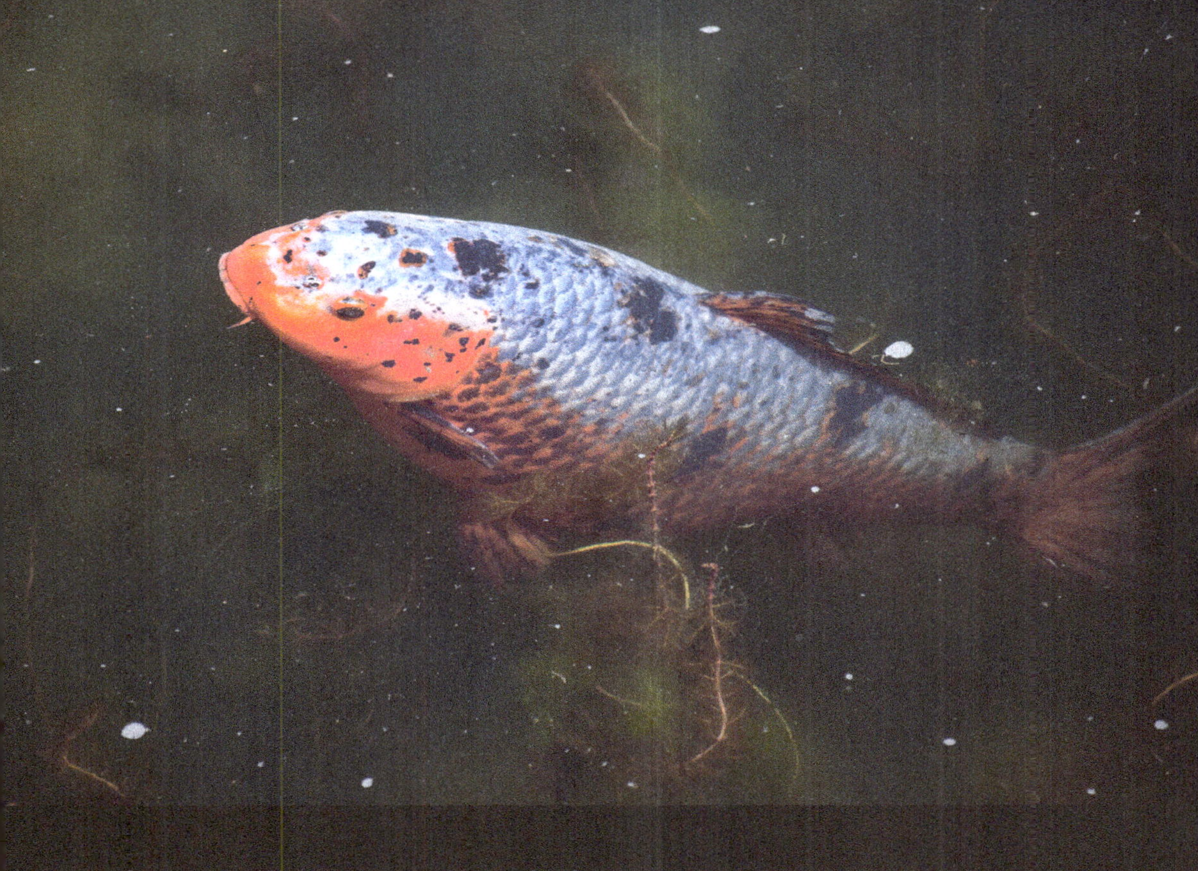

When spring warmed the waters, King Koi
emerged so hungry he was sure he had lost a lot
of weight during hibernation. His pals did not
have the heart to tell him a two-year hibernation
would have done him some good.

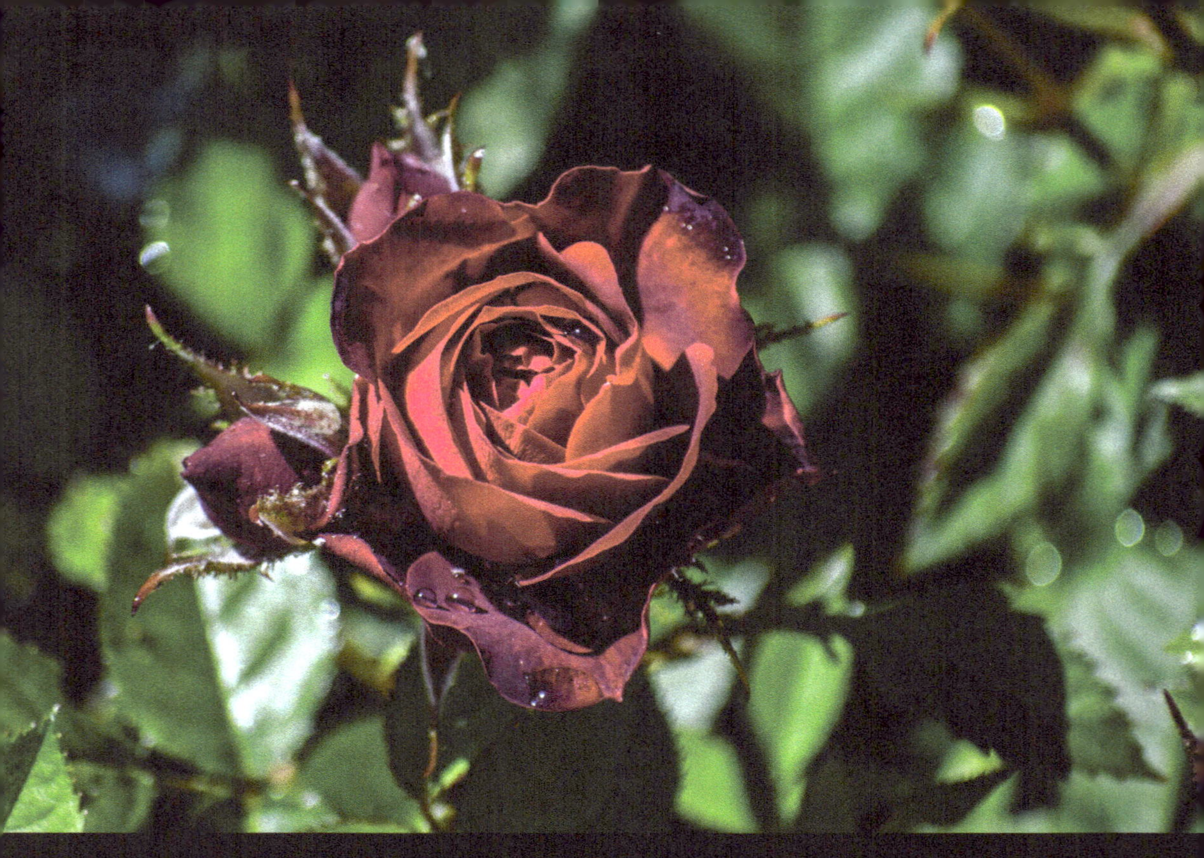

Rain kissed Rose and left a tracing of his love for her. She welcomed Sun's warmth but was sad to lose the last, gentle touch of Rain.

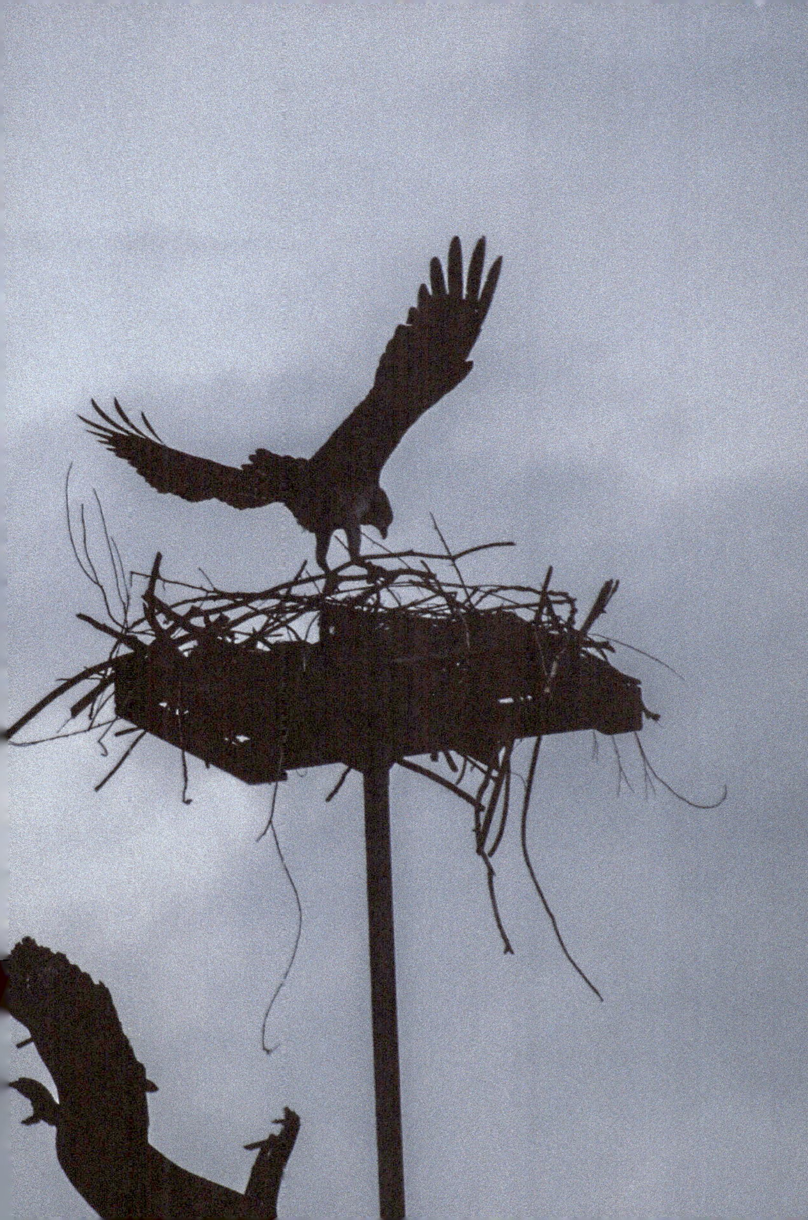

It had been a long day, but Father Osprey made one more flight to gather nesting materials. He wanted this year's home to be safe and secure for the eggs his mate would soon lay.

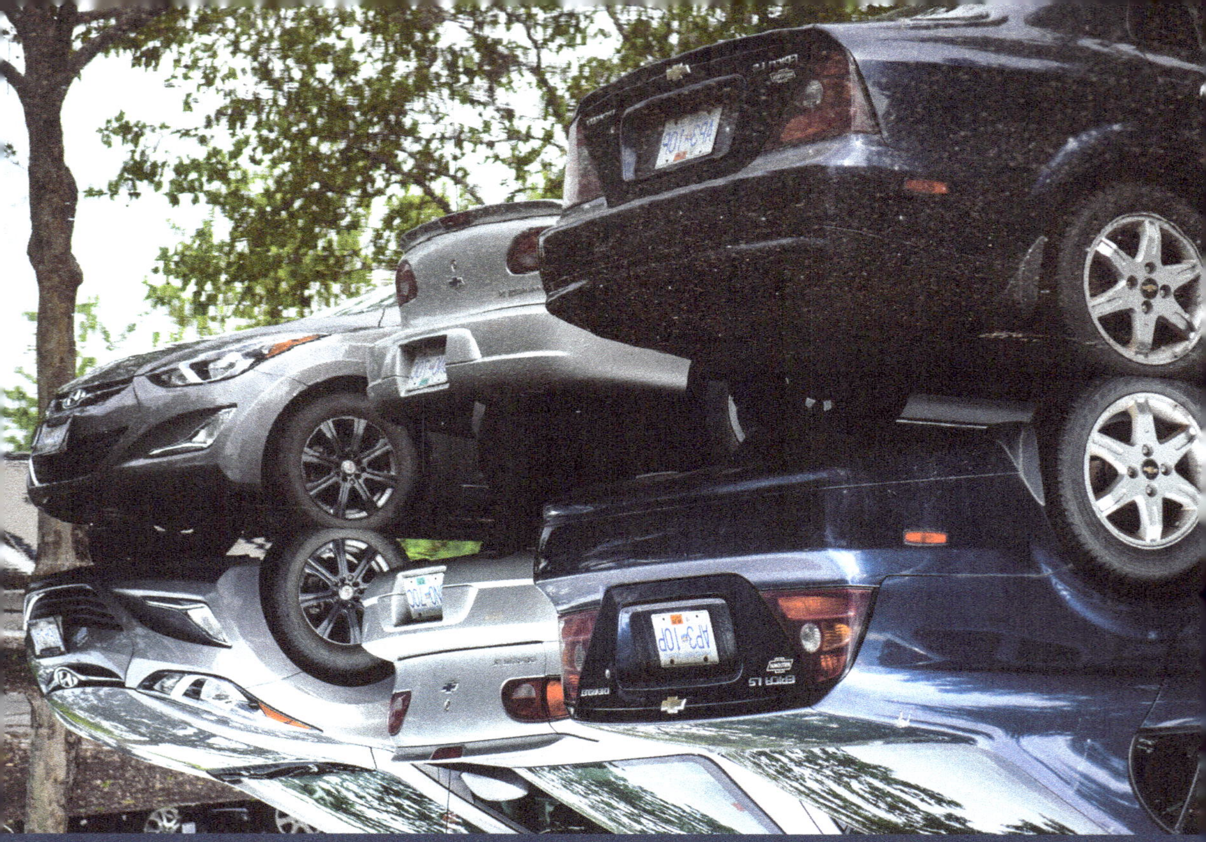

Wind and flood waters were cooperating with the cars, but that darned pollen was threatening to give away their joke.

[The joke is easier to see if you turn the book upside down.]

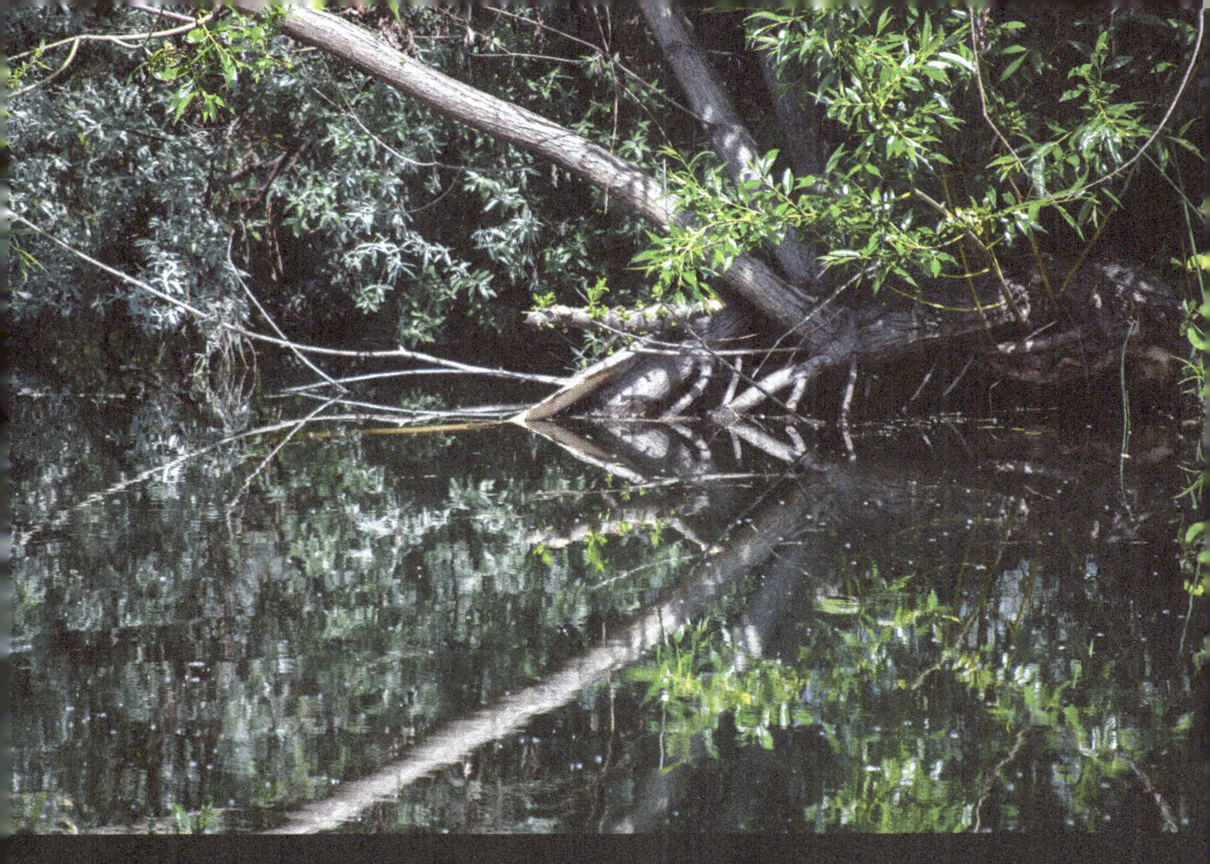

Some days Willow was irritated with Beaver's gnawing on her. But with Water high and Wind silent, Beaver's latest work created beautiful heart reflections. Willow wondered if that was accidental or if Beaver had become an artist.

Big Blues
gazed
admiringly
on Little
Whites.
"They are so
much more
delicate,"
they sighed.
Little Whites
looked up at
Big Blues.
"They are so
much
brighter,"
they
thought.

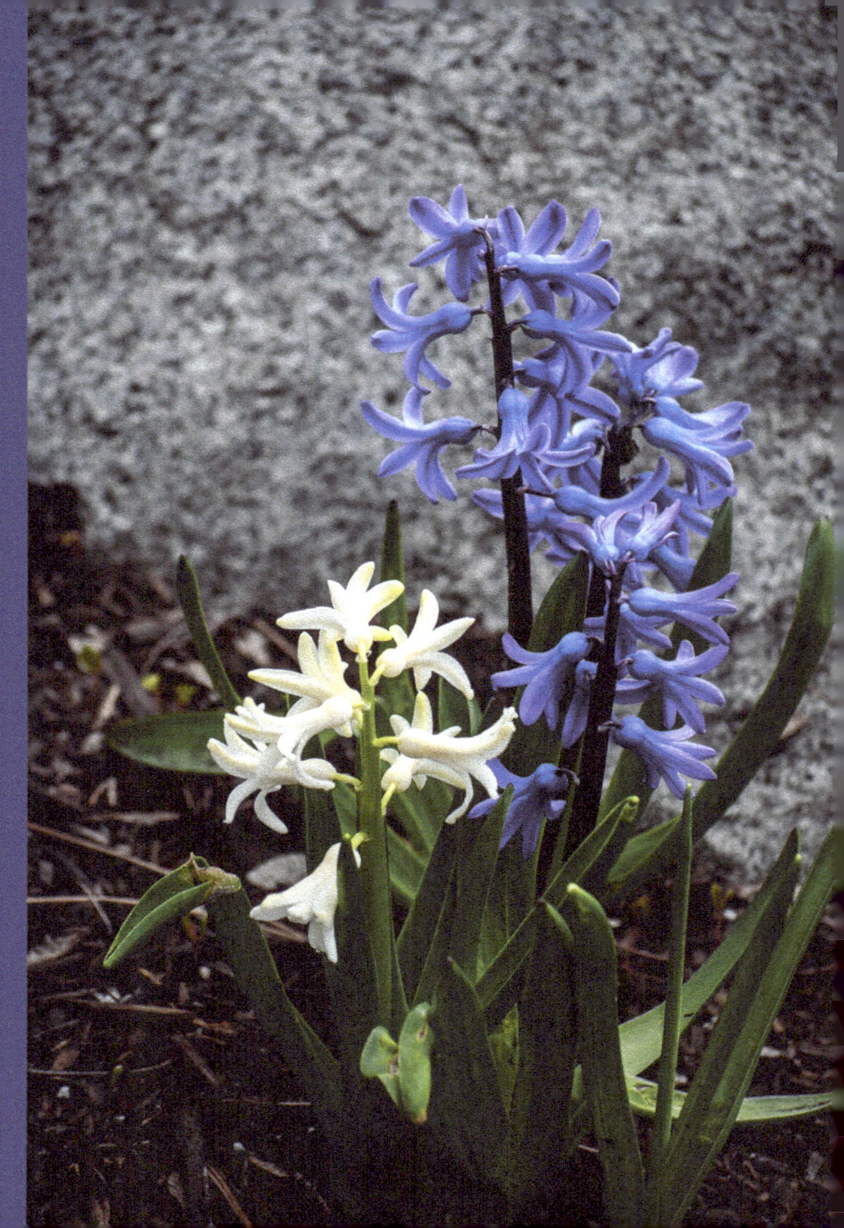

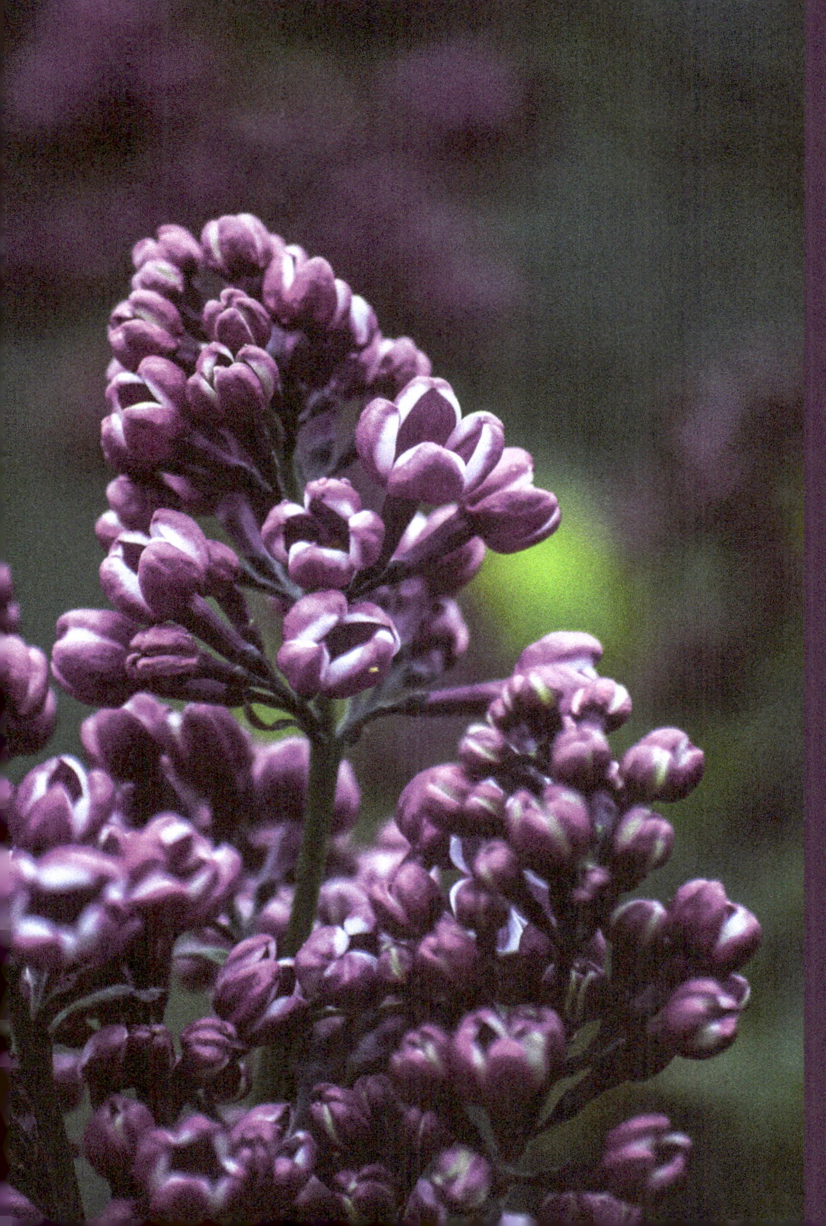

Lilacs knew they were gorgeous and fragrant. They just wished humans would keep their stupid dogs from peeing on their feet.

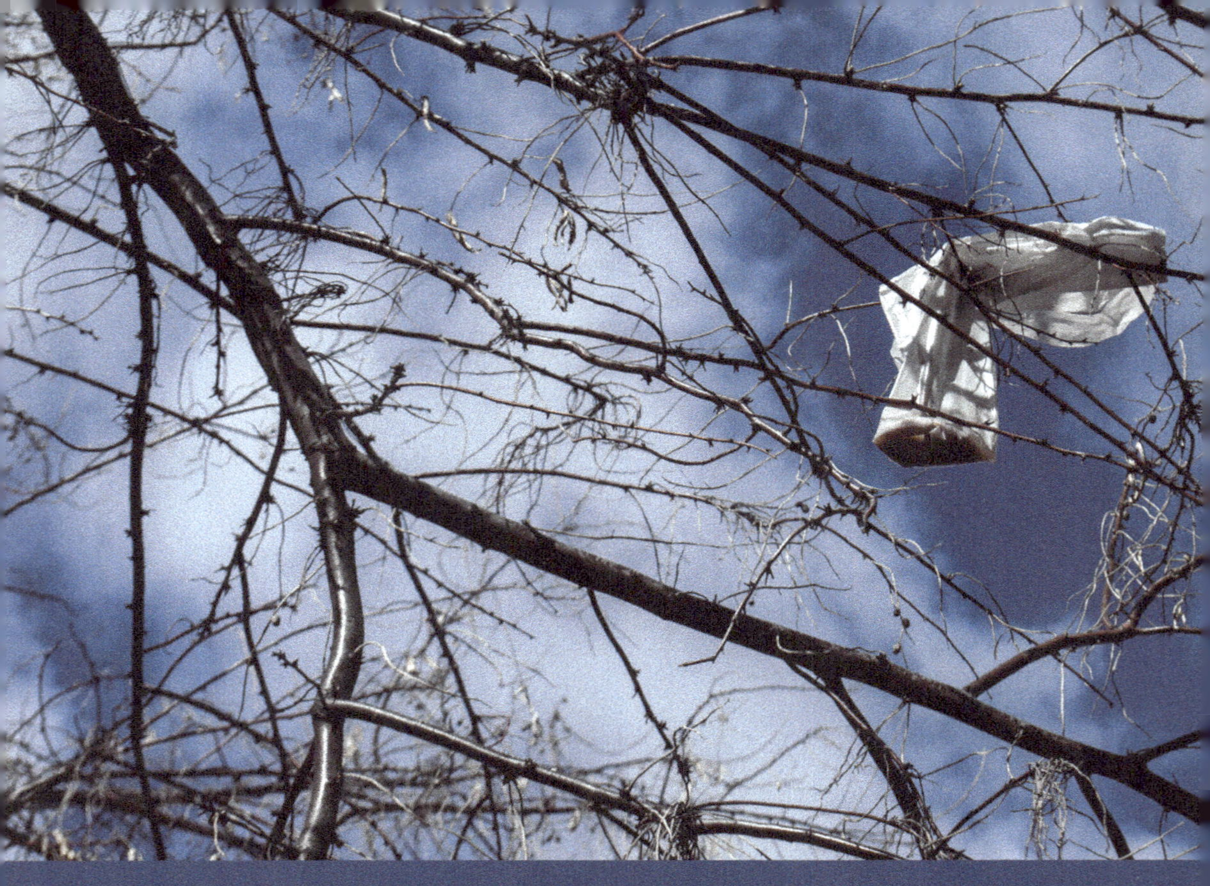

Bread's day started out fine. A human put him in a plastic bag and took him for a walk. Then things changed. Wind grabbed the bag and flung it into a tree. Bread wondered how it would all end.

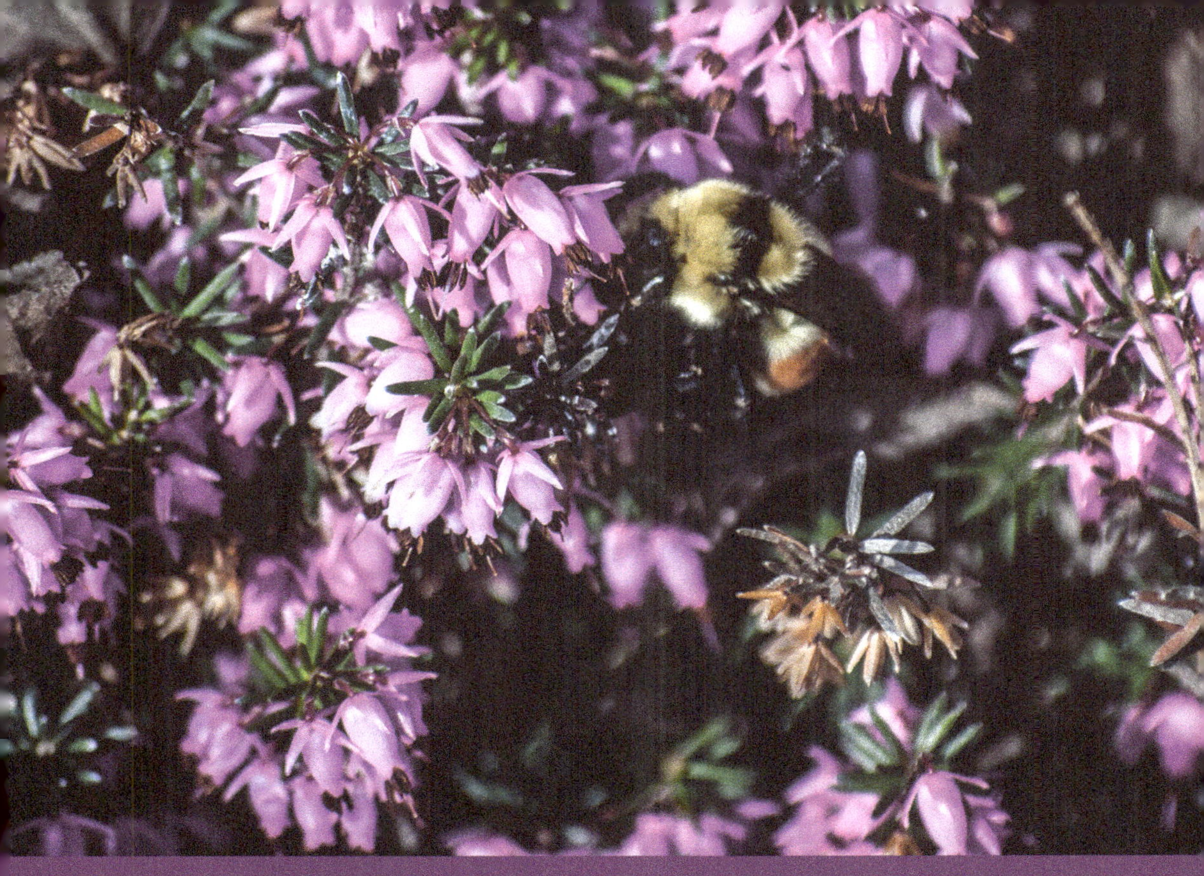

"You're late," grumbled Bee. "Now I have to work hard to catch up." Heather ignored Bee's grumbles. She was not in charge of Weather and knew her blossoms were her best ever.

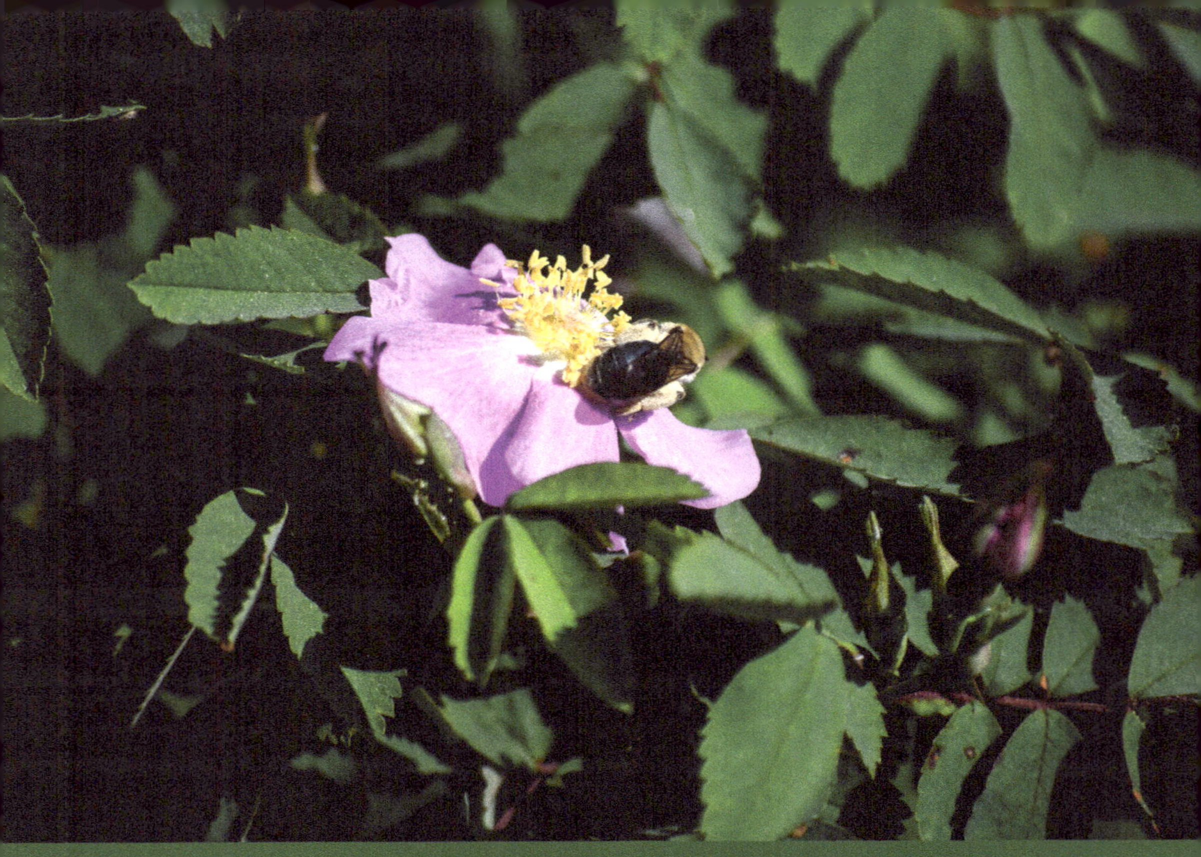

Bee's legs grew heavy with pollen. He was tempted to return to the hive, but, when he left one delicious rose, he saw another. They were too alluring to resist.

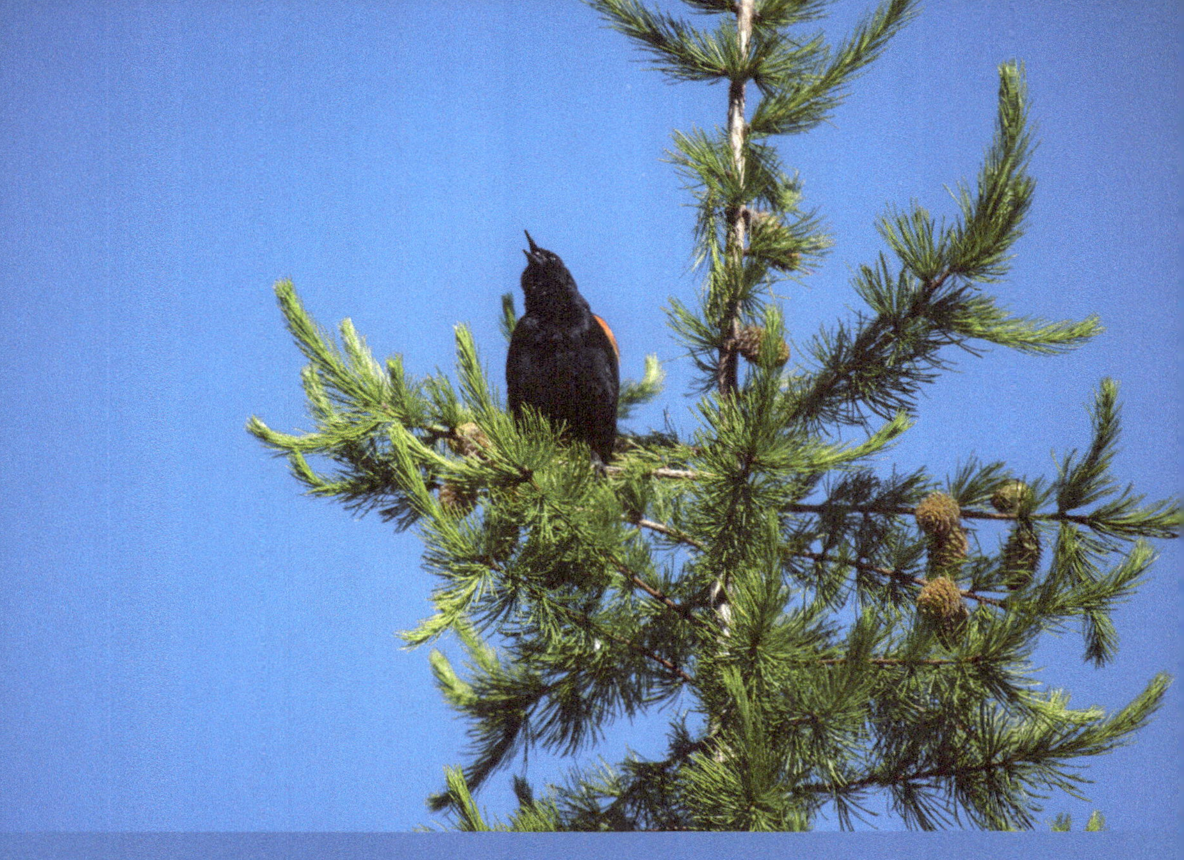

"Oh, what a beautiful morning," sang Red-winged Blackbird. Humans thought they had written the song, but RWB knew his ancestors had composed the music long before Rogers and Hammerstein were even born.

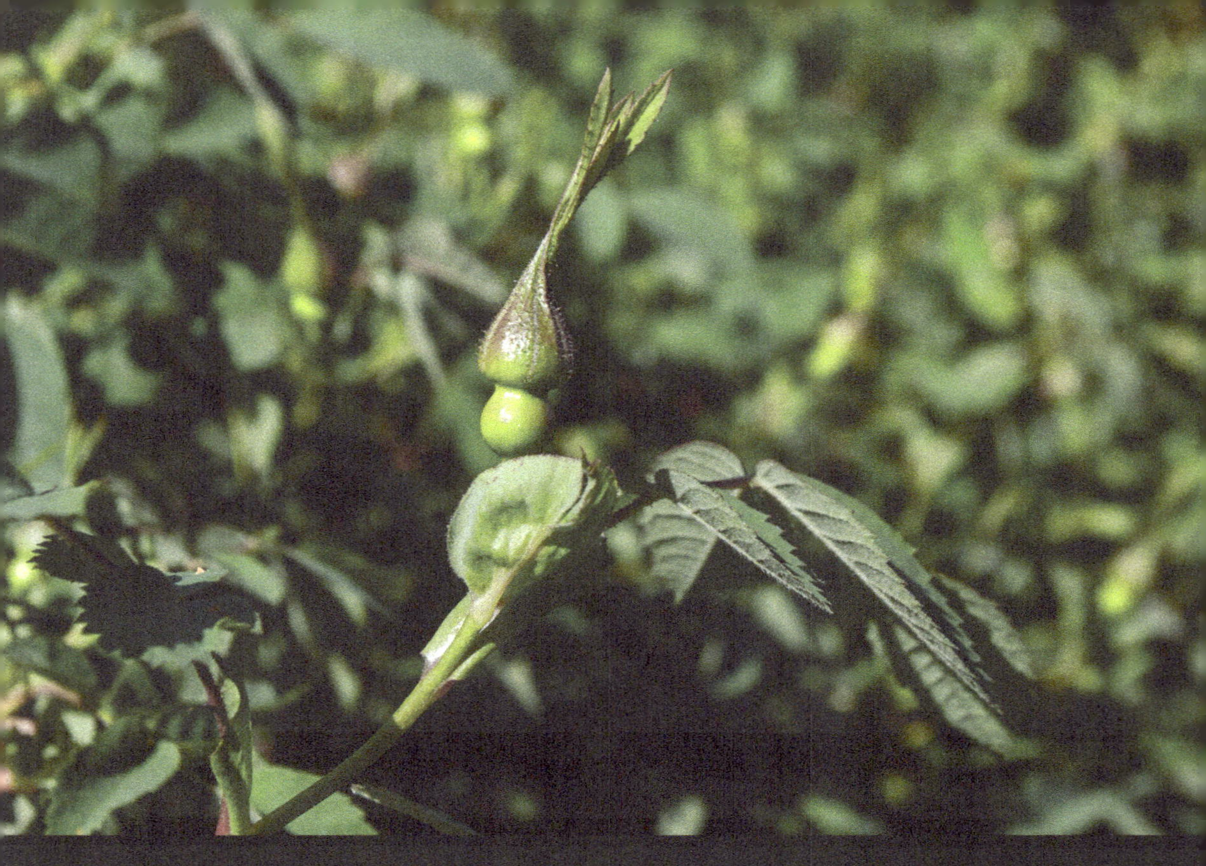

The adventure was just beginning. She could feel herself swelling and wondered what she would become when her top burst open.

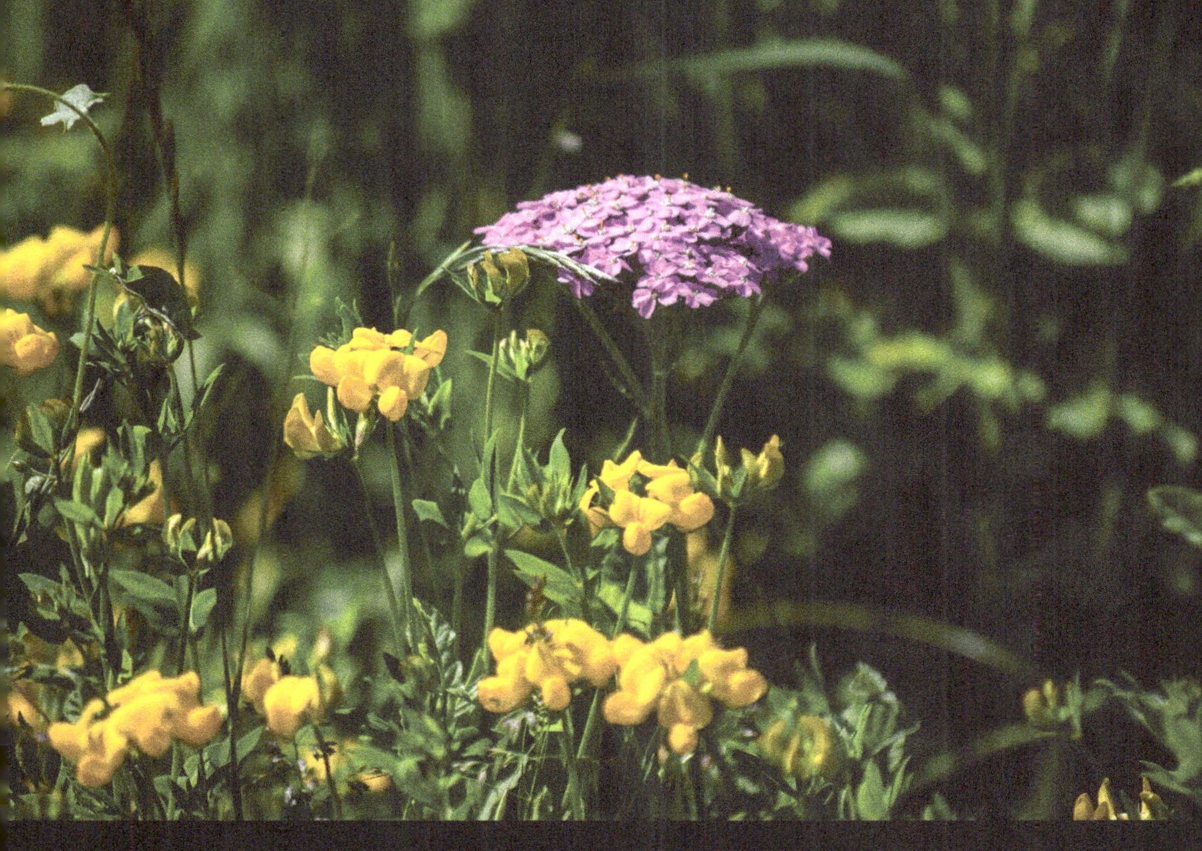

Yarrow loved her noisy neighbors. They were loudly yellow and cheerfully gossiped about all the happenings in the marsh. For the quieter Yarrow, they were first-rate entertainment.

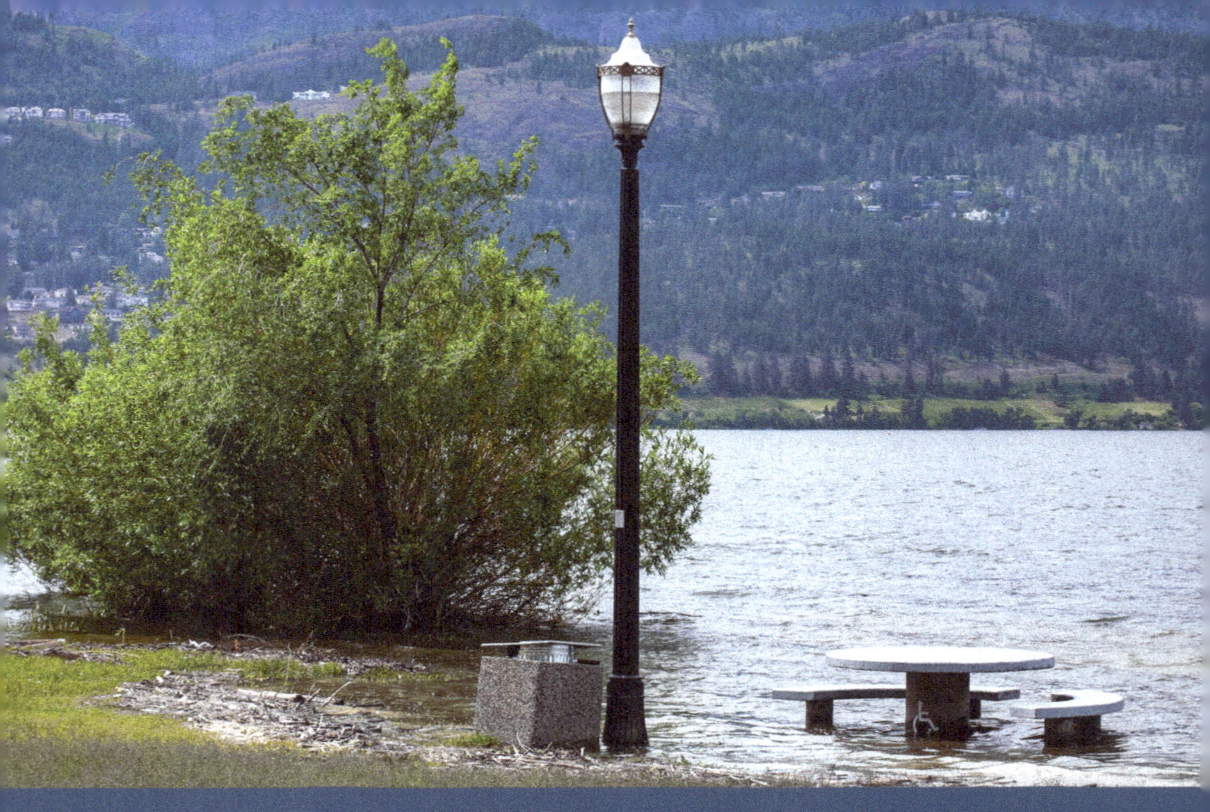

Picnic Table missed her wheelchair pals and wished Flood Waters would go away. Garbage can popped out of his bin, trying to cheer her up.

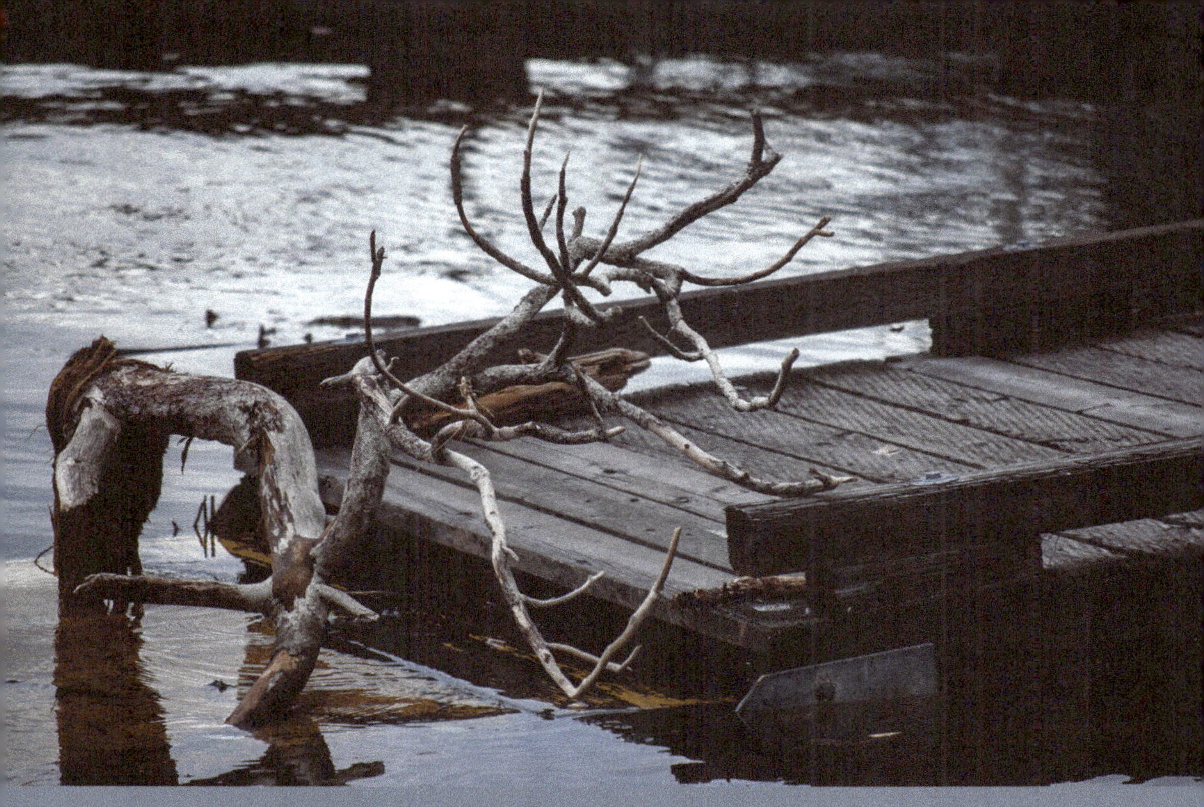

"So I was hanging around on a beach when Water swept me across the lake, and I ended up here." Dock was polite to the log but was a little tired of chatty newcomers washing up on him. He longed for normal water levels and summer boats.

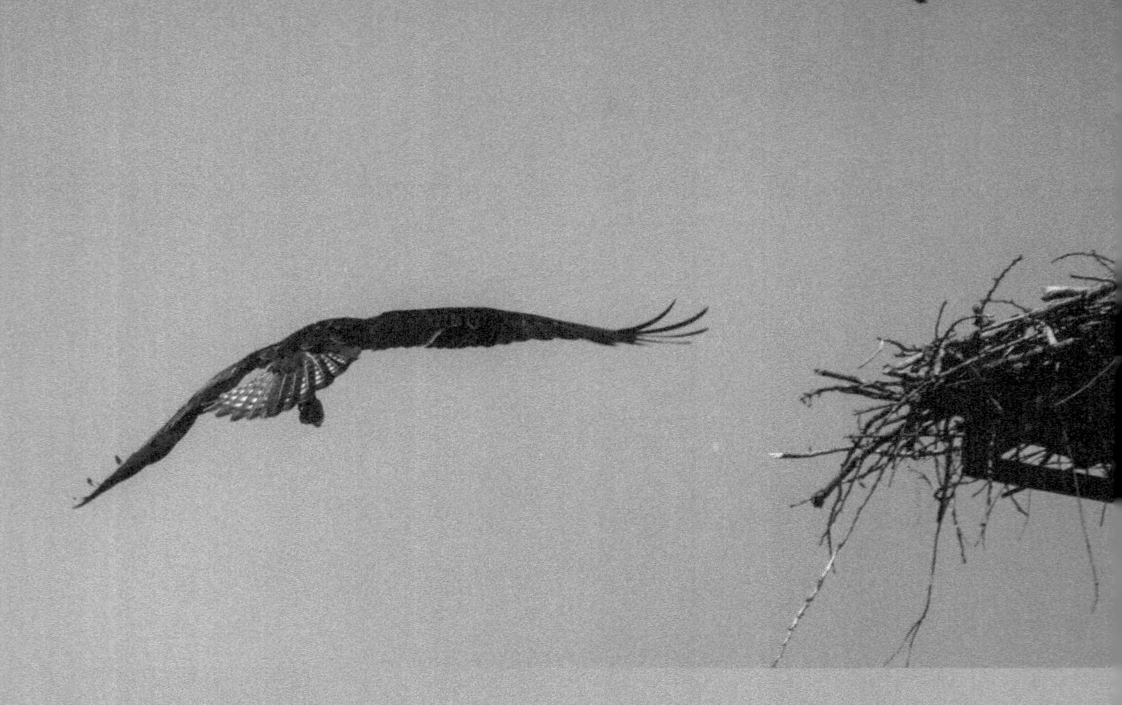

Nothing made Blackbird happier than to dive bomb Osprey as he flew home with dinner. Today had been particularly satisfying.

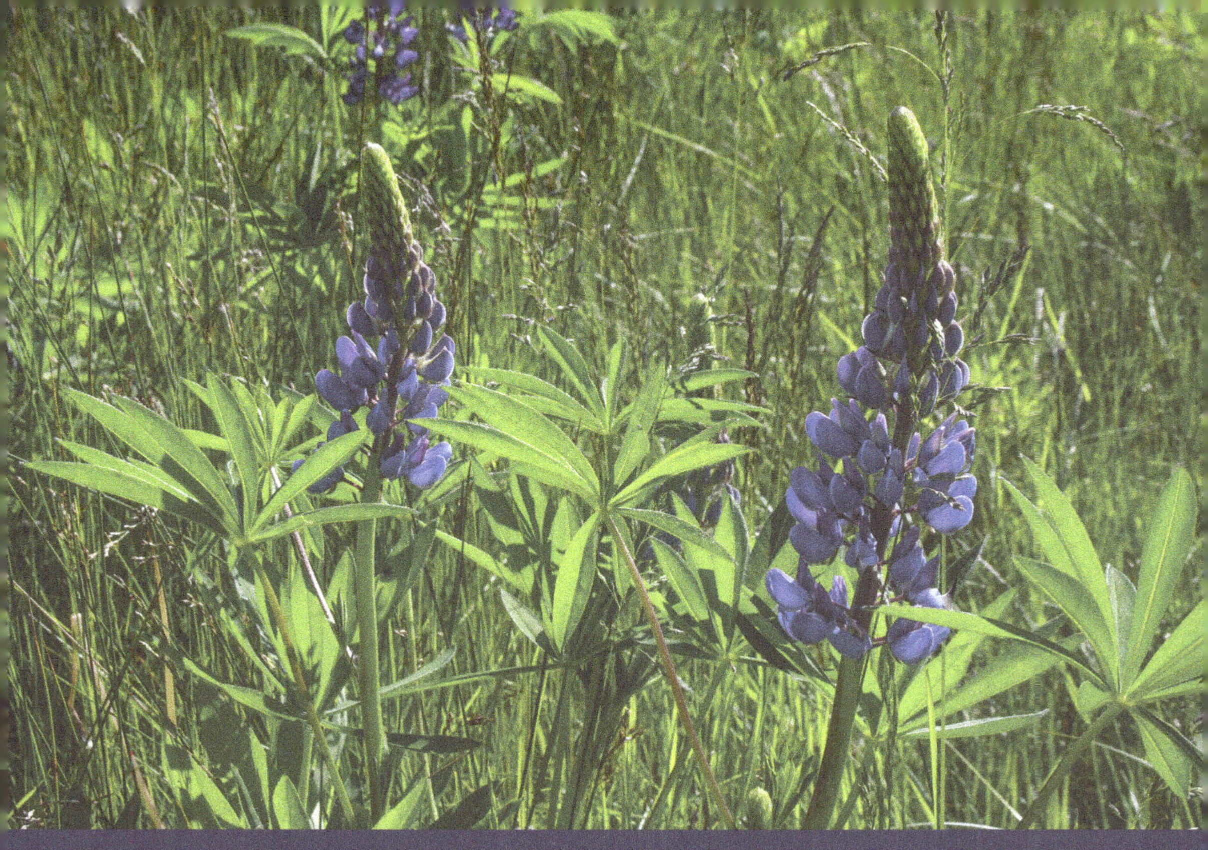

"I believe she's flirting with me," thought Lupine, catching sight of the delicate stalk leaning his way. After a winter underground, wondering what was in the world above, he was suddenly shy and uncertain how to act.

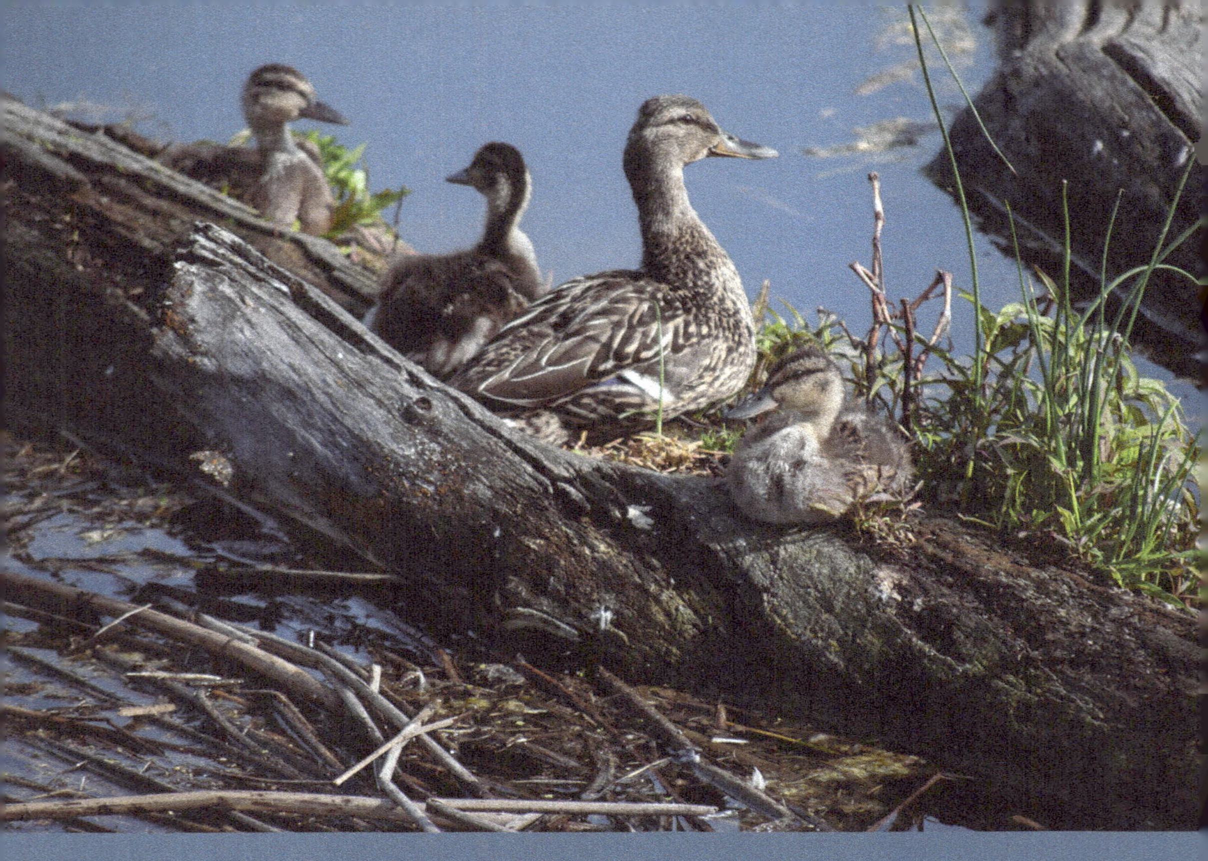

Ducklings watched as their mother lifted her head and turned an eye toward the human. "It's OK," she quacked. "They're mostly harmless, but keep an eye on them. They can be fickle."

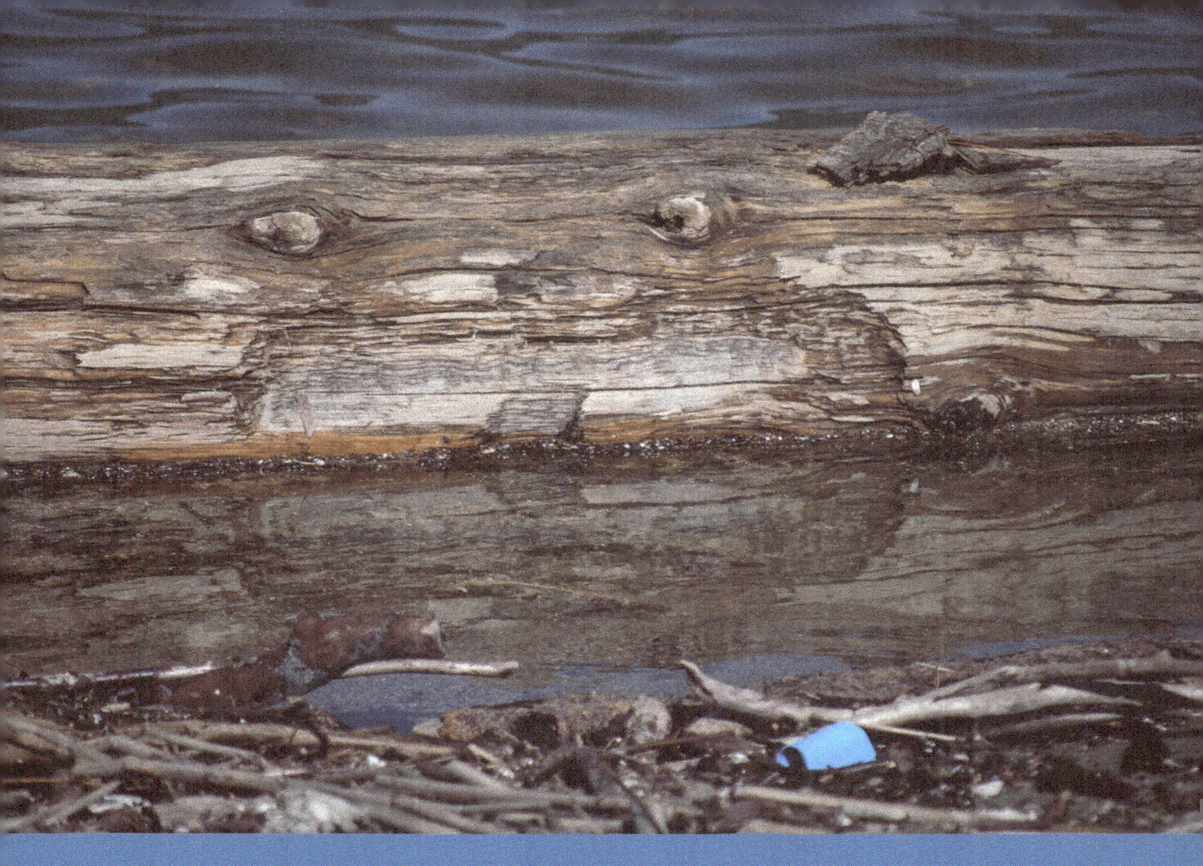

Frog Log escaped the log boom destined for a sawmill, but he could not escape the wind that washed him ashore. He missed his freedom and hoped whatever lay ahead would be as much fun as floating.

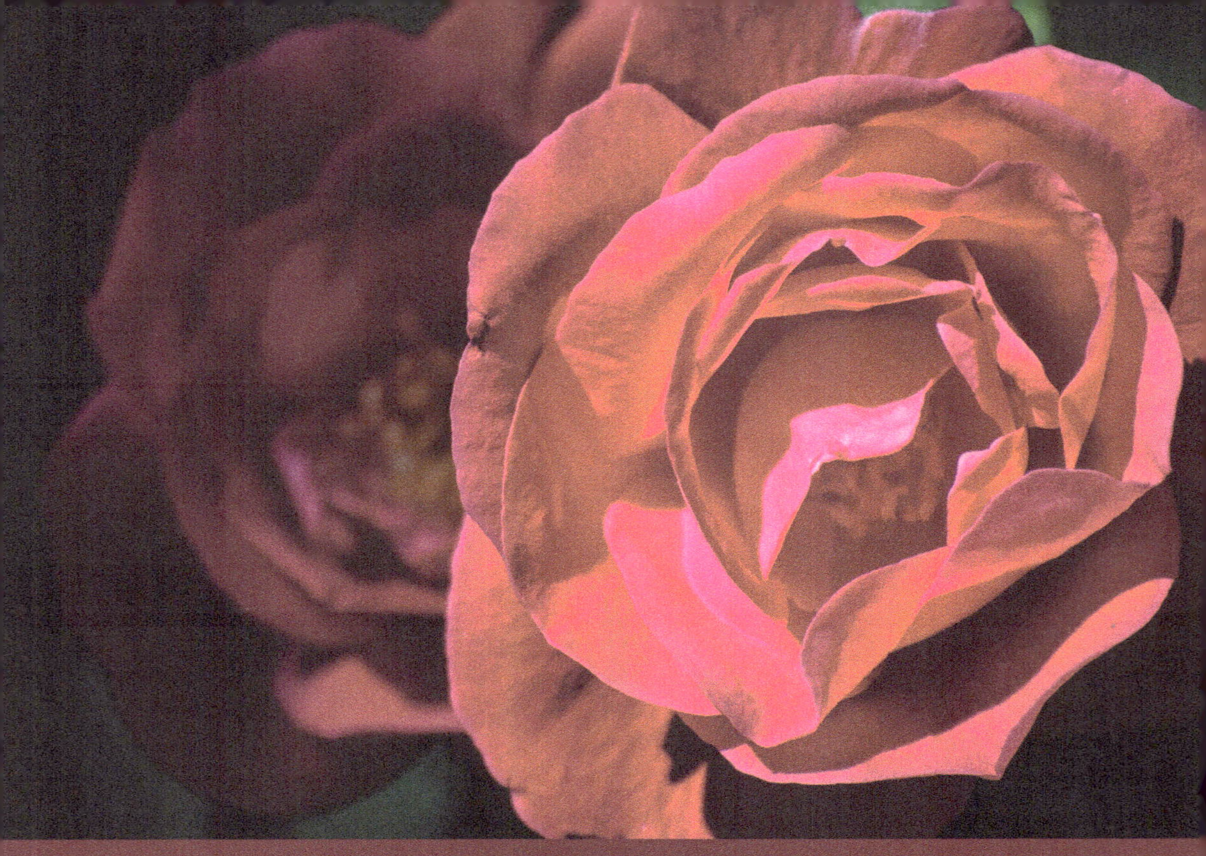

Rose volunteered to be Leader on the bush. Her cousins were a little jealous at first. Then they realized people who stopped to stare at her also admired the rest of them.

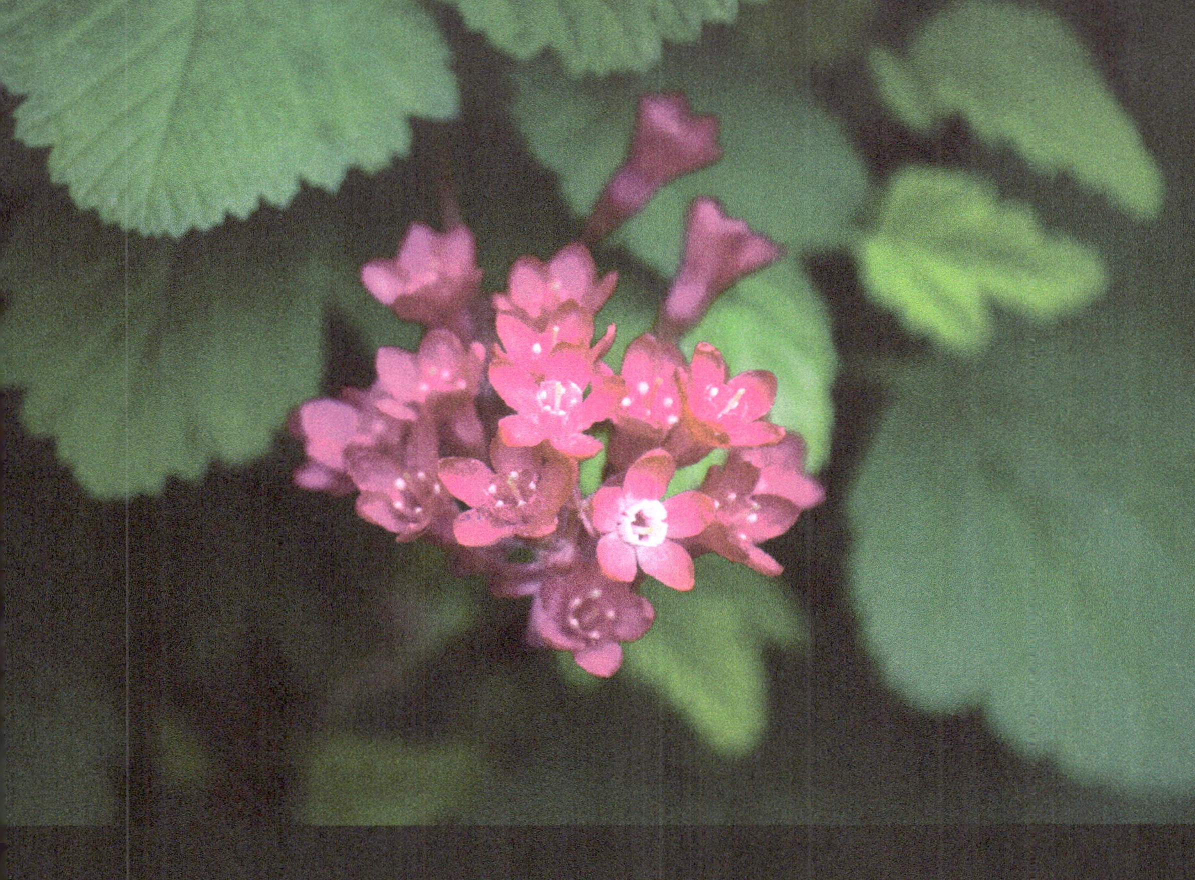

Last year Molly hid among her sisters, afraid she was not pretty enough. This year she flung aside her fears and shone brightly.

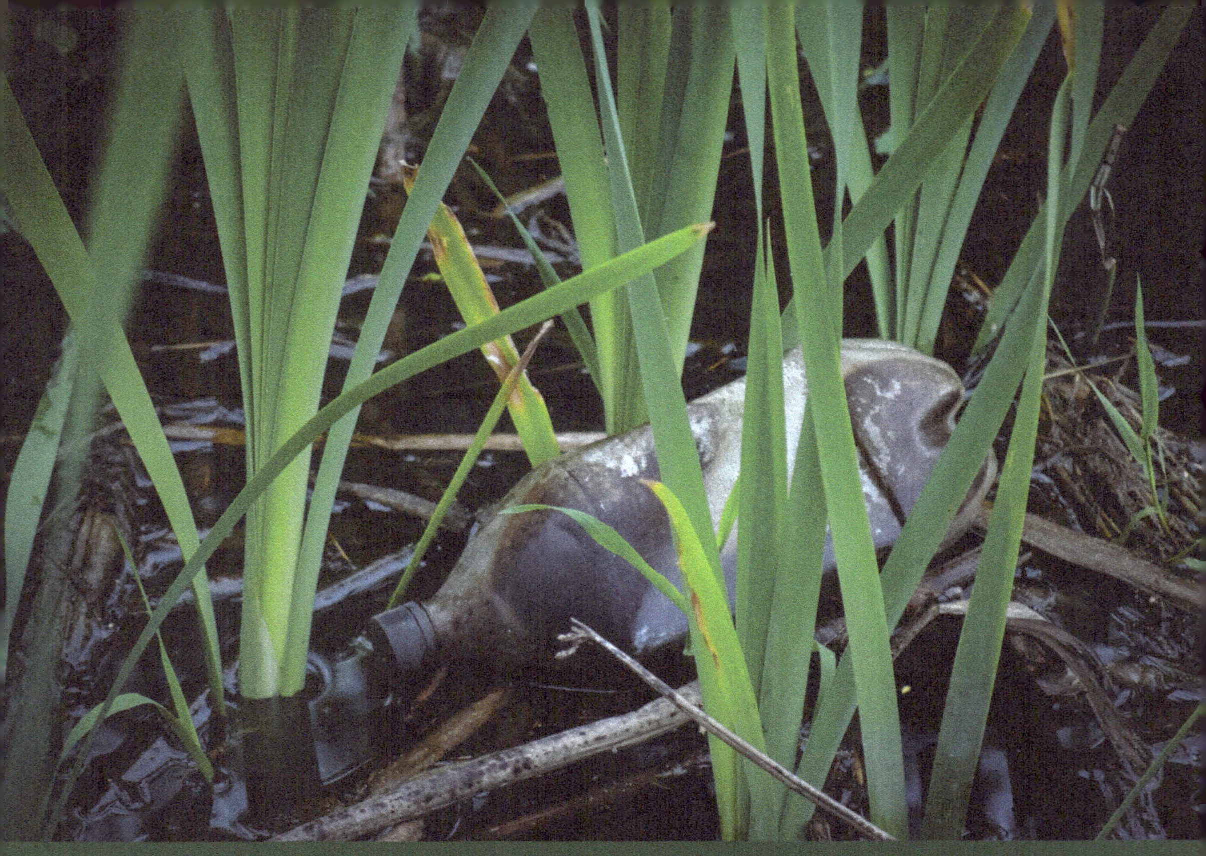

Just this morning tiny ducklings made her laugh as they clambered over her slippery sides. It eased the disappointment of being tossed away like some useless object.

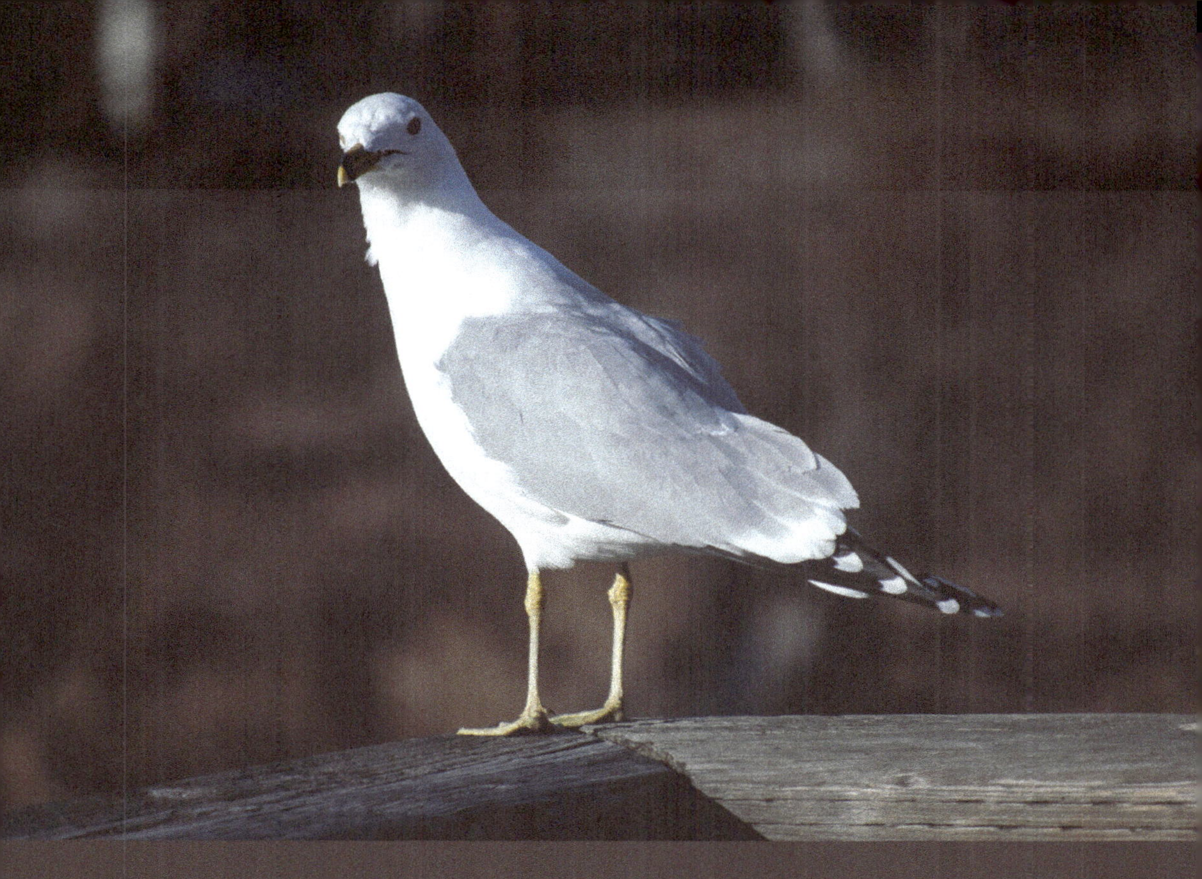

Gull looked at the mallards, contemplated the Canada geese, noted the coots. "Seriously?" he thought. "They call themselves birds? Oh, I know they migrate long distances, but they lack my soaring grace. Still, they are mildly amusing."

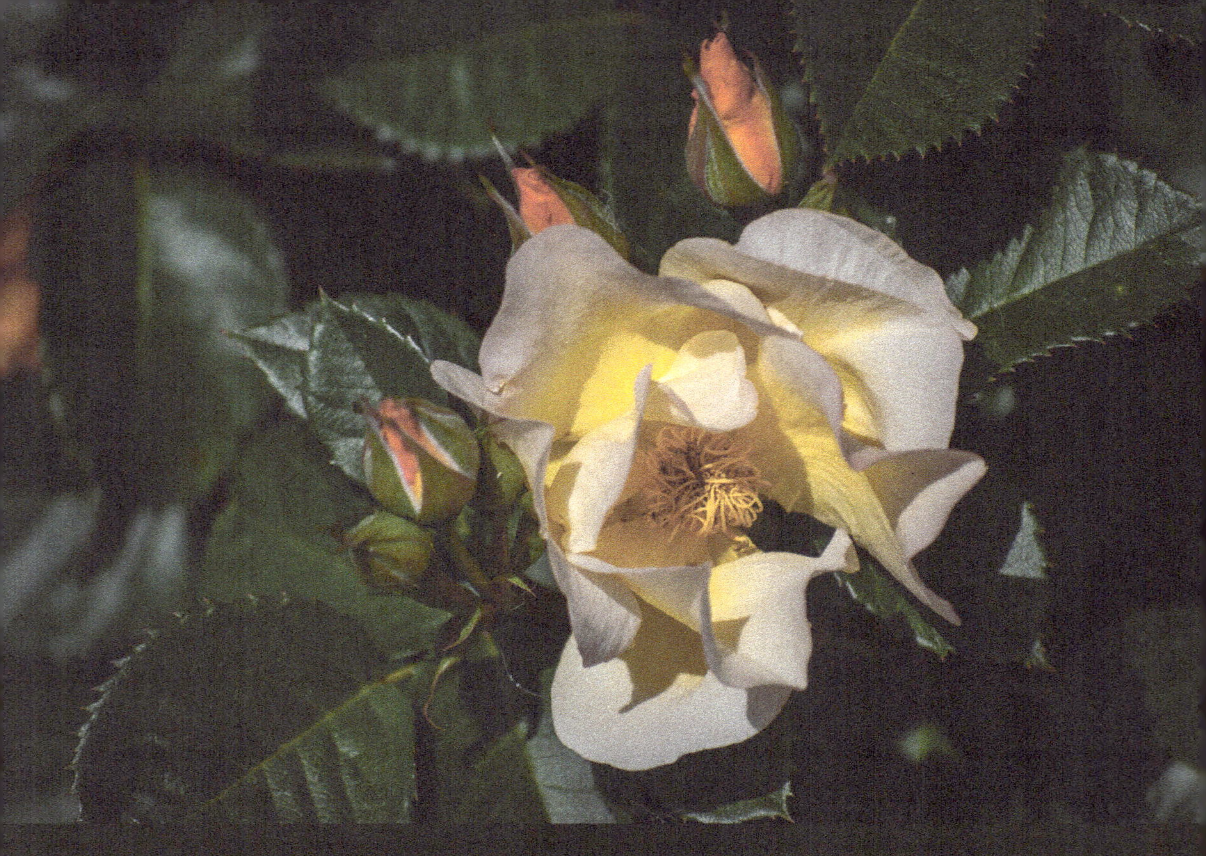

Rose could not wait for her cousins to grow big enough to play with. The only thing that worried her was that she might be too old and tired by the time they blossomed.

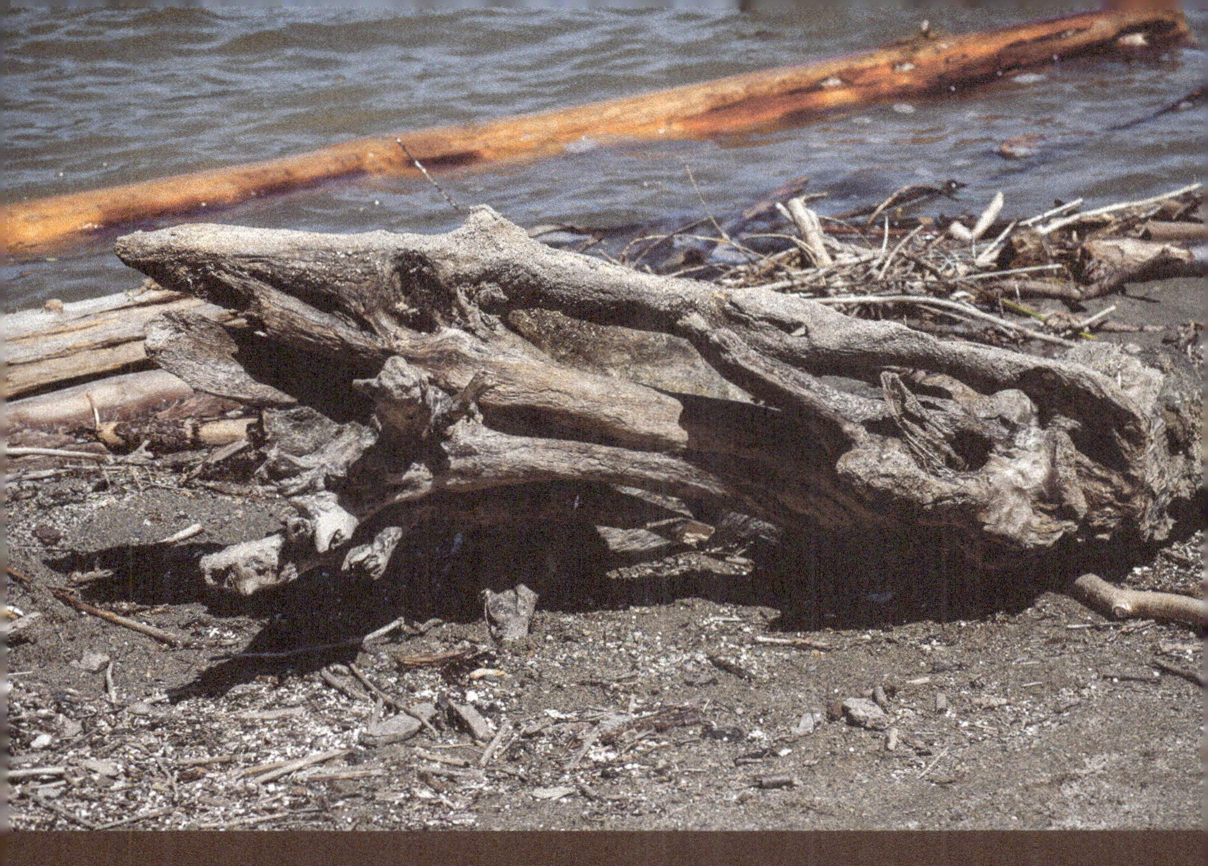

"Boy, you sure are orange," Crocodile Stump said to Log. "It's the latest style in floodwear," said Log sarcastically. Stump completely missed the sarcasm but could not think of a polite answer so fell silent.

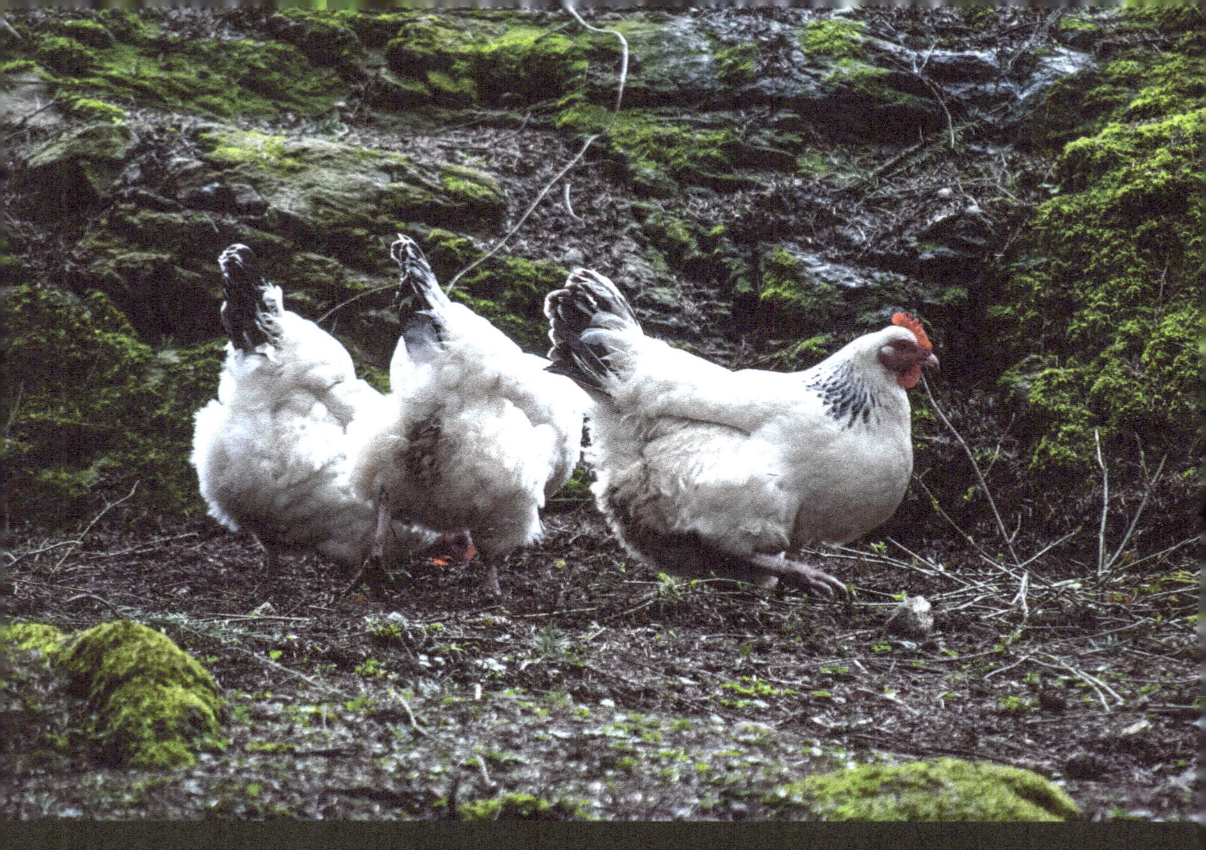

Henrietta dropped a bit of frippery. As soon as the girls turned to check it out, Henrietta ran to eat the best of the seed the human visitor had tossed their way. The ruse worked every time.

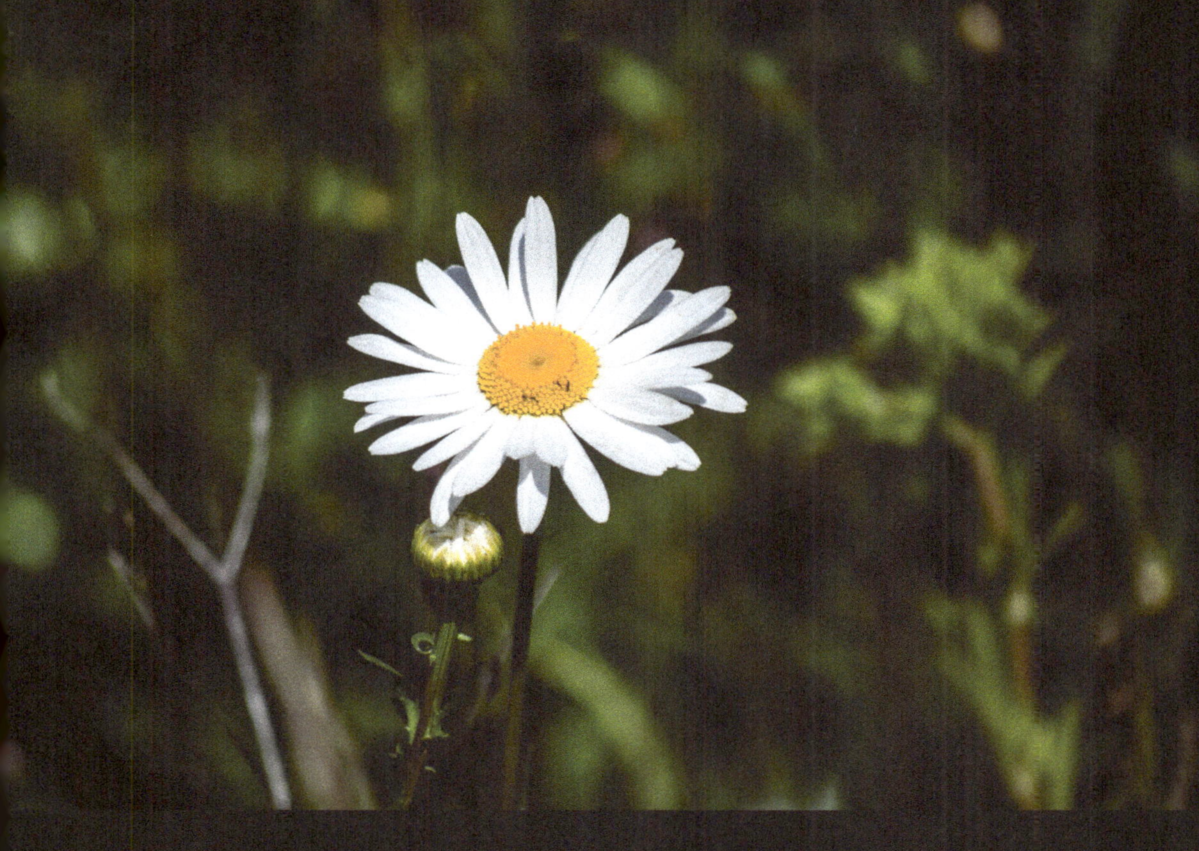

Sometimes Daisy pretended she was all alone in the world, just to see what it would feel like. It was never as much fun as having plenty of relatives nearby, even when they were irritating.

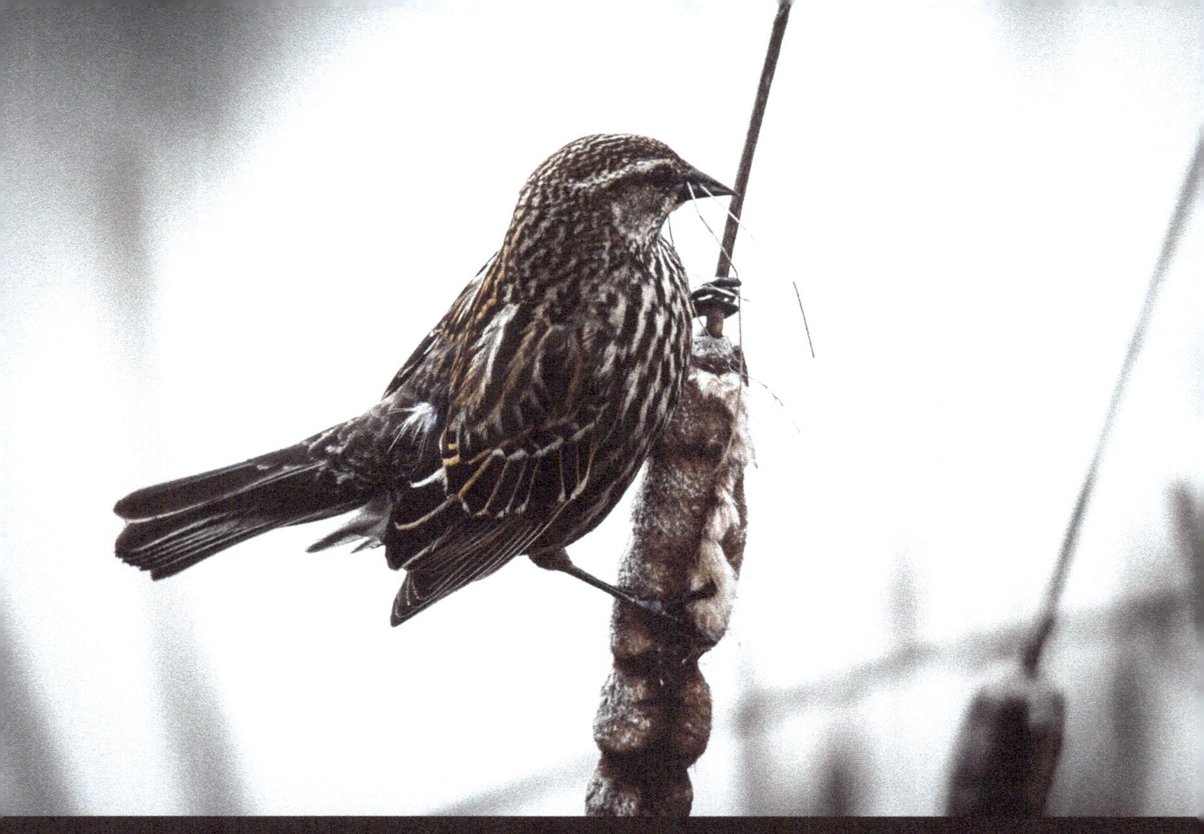

She paused in her nest building. She knew her mate would guard her fiercely once the chicks hatched. But she couldn't help wishing he were more interested in bringing materials for this year's home.

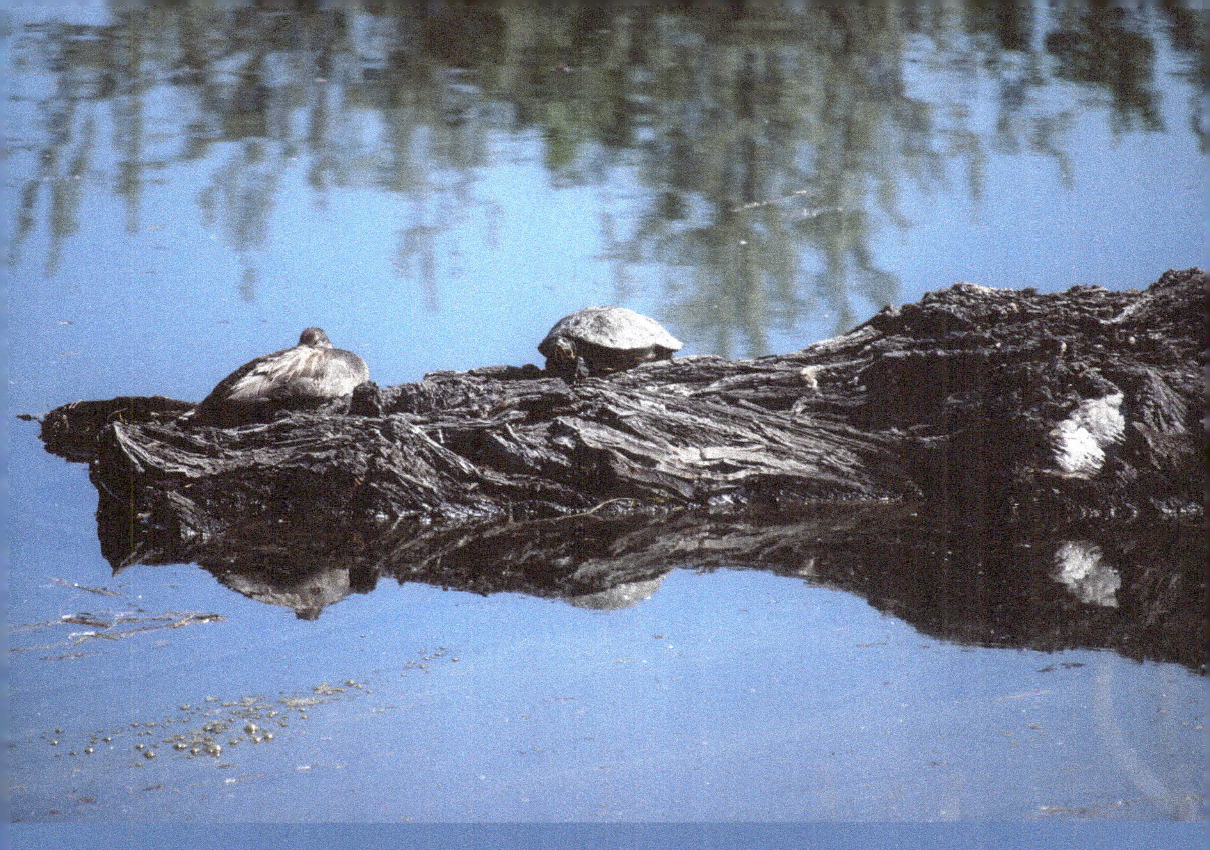

As the flood waters rose, all the best resting spots disappeared. Small turtles left in search of better homes. Old Turtle was lonely, with only a few Gadwall ducks for company. Not one of them knew the good stories from the marsh.

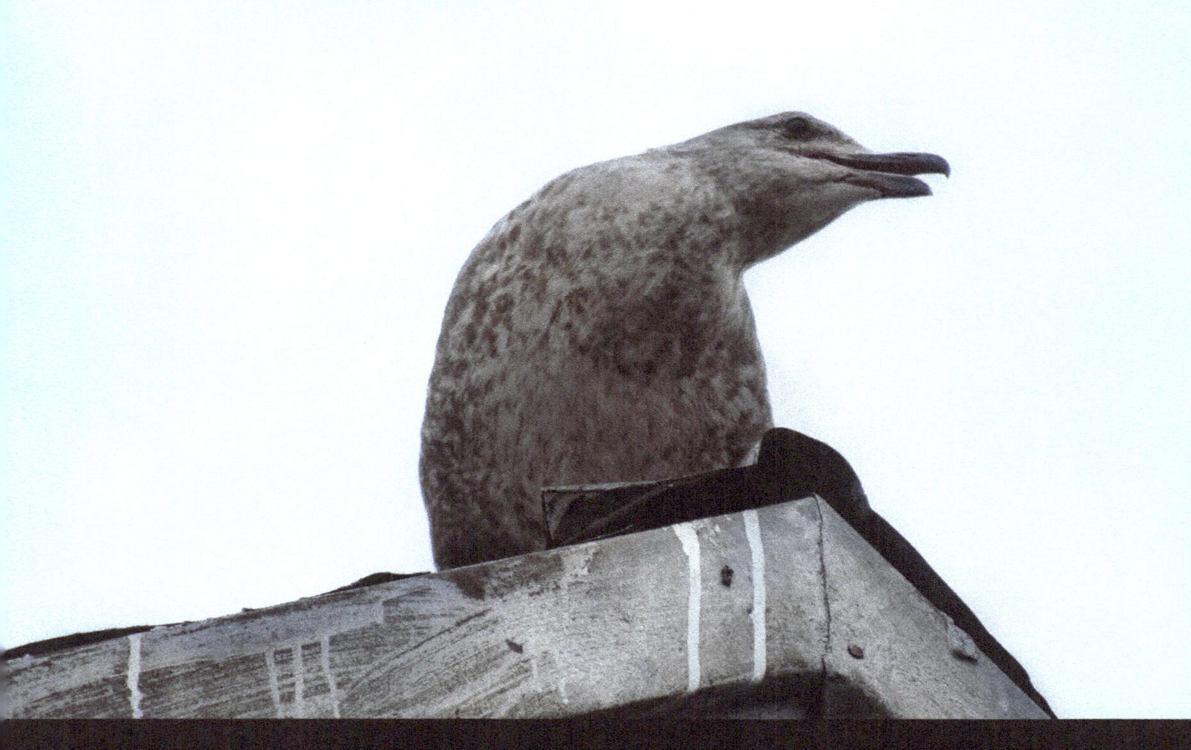

"Wow! Did they see me dive? Did they watch me catch the updraft? Are they impressed? Do they think I'm special? Will they let me hang out with them?" Junior was thrilled to be grown enough to be on his own, but he had some insecurities.

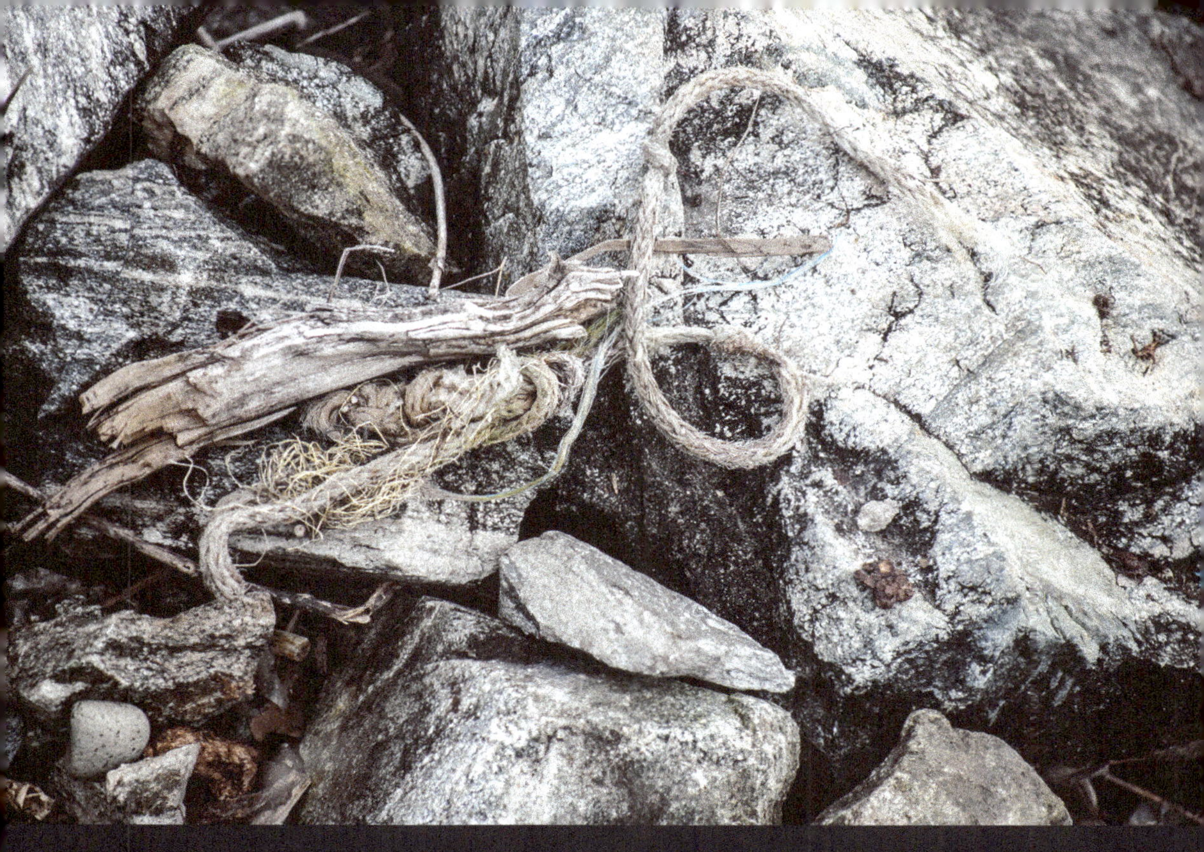

Rope and stick met after a storm deposited them atop the stones. They talked about the weather until they felt relaxed with each other. Then they dived into the deeper waters of friendship.

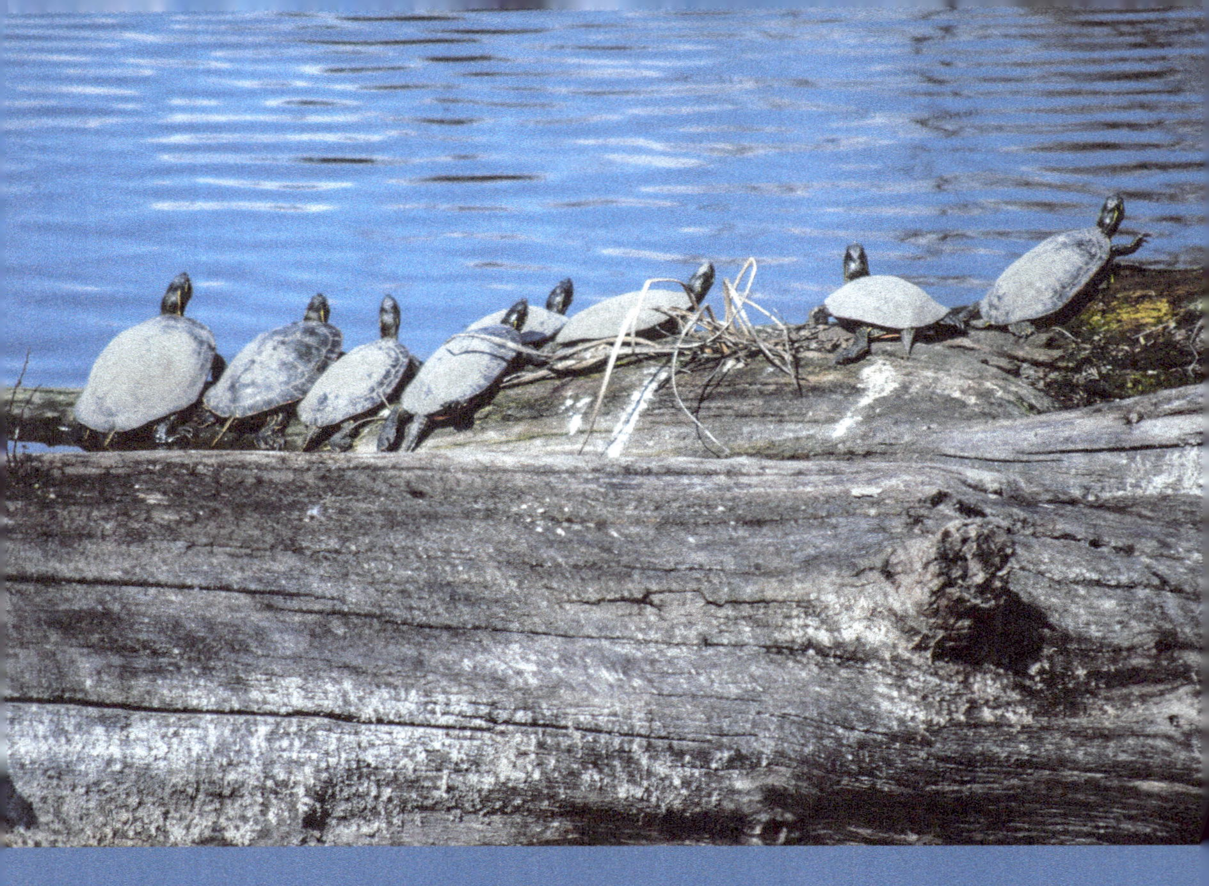

"Look up," said Turtle Leader. They all did. It was a sobering moment for Turtle Leader, who suddenly felt the weight of responsibility rest on his carapace.

ABOUT THE AUTHOR

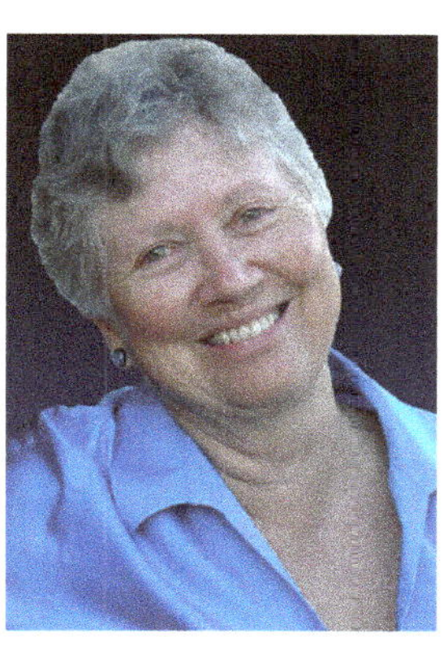

Cathryn Wellner is a writer, photographer and storyteller living in Kelowna, British Columbia, Canada. Her recent books include:

In the Shelter of Each Other
The Disappearing Pumpkin Choir
That Tree Talked to Me
Parts of Me Are Still Amazing
Hope Wins
Feisty Aging
In the Hug of Hills
Millie's Feathered Foster Family
Turkey Baby and the Hungry Hawk
Turkey Baby Finds Her Magic

You can find links to these and her other books at cathrynwellner.com. Contact her at cathryn@cathrynwellner.com or 778-478-2760. Her photographs can be found on her Web site, as well as on Facebook and Instagram.

BE A BOOK REVIEW ANGEL

If you enjoyed this book, please post a review on Amazon or Goodreads. Share it with friends and rave about it on social media. You can contact the author at cathryn@cathrynwellner.com.

Authors rely on their readers to help spread the word about books they like. People who review books are special kinds of reader angels. I guarantee when you review this book, or any other book that has given you pleasure in any way, you'll feel those wings poking out your back. Look closely in the mirror, and you might even see a halo.

Credits

Fonts used on cover and some interior pages: Saltash, Sun Kissed, and Salt & Pepper. Font used in stories: Bw Surco. Logo font: Ed's Market. Mask on dedication page by Ghostly Pixels. All fonts and graphic elements are licensed through DesignCuts.

Text and photographs by Cathryn Wellner. The book was designed in Photoshop.

Thank you to the creative people who designed the unique fonts and elements incorporated in this book. I continually learn from you.

Note re flood stories: My Canadian home—Kelowna, British Columbia—experienced record-breaking water levels in spring and early summer 2017. I found it shattering to watch waters devour beaches, float away docks, and drown blackbird nests. As soon as the flooding ended, fires broke out all around the province, which was declared a disaster area for the first time since the awful fires of 2003. My worries crept into the photographs and stories from that time.

Small Scale Stories are, at heart, about loving and safekeeping our beautiful planet. Let's cherish the blue ball we live on.

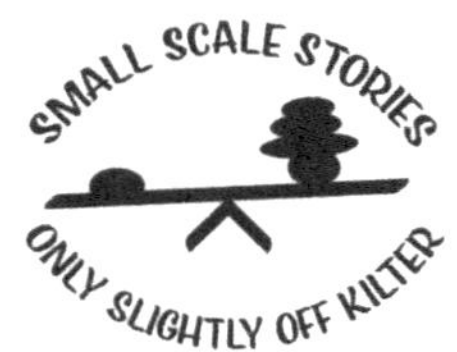